Managing Microsoft Windows 7 through Group Policies

A Pocket Guide for Administrators

Vivek Nayyar

http://www.pctips3000.com

Managing Microsoft Windows 7 through Group Policies - A Pocket Guide for Administrators by Vivek Nayyar

*This book is dedicated to my loving dad **Mr. V. K. Nayyar***

whose abilities have always inspired me to do something different

*and in the loving memory of my mom **Late Mrs. Indu Nayyar***

who always wanted me to rise and shine.

- Vivek Nayyar

Acknowledgements

I am thankful to all those who devoted their time and shared their experiences during the creation of this book. Entire credit for the success of this book goes to them only.

Avijit Palival
Network Engineer

Tarun Kandpal
Systems Engineer
ICA

Csaba Kissi
PCTIPS3000
Site Owner

Irshad Alam
Team Lead, Ship Corp.
Kolkata

Kunwer Shoeb Rana
T.G.T.
Natural Science

Lou Cordova
Medical Administrator
Toronto, Ontario

Navneet Mehta
State Head
R.G. Global

Preeti Rai
Govt. of India
Lucknow

Rakesh Tiwari
Dealing Assistant
ESIC, Govt. of India

Riza Rosal
Supervisor
Kuwait City

Swagata Bharali
Network Support Engg. Microsoft

About the Author

Vivek Nayyar

Vivek Nayyar has 8+ years' experience in academic and corporate IT training and systems administration on Microsoft and Virtualization platforms. Today he works as Senior Windows Administrator and Chief Editor at PCTIPS3000. He also works as LAN Consultant and provides remote support to various IT oriented organizations around the globe. He has written several IT related blogs and articles on Microsoft and VMware and has been working on Windows since 2001. He is an author of the book "Microsoft Windows 7 - A Complete How-To Guide".

Table of Contents

Introduction

This book can serve as a pocket guide to the IT professionals (especially administrators and desktop engineers) to make their daily IT related tasks easier.

This pocket guide is written keeping in mind that the administrators who are new to the industry and the students who are at their initial learning stages may get benefited with the contents that this guide contains. This guide contains simple How-To tips along with the descriptions explaining which GPO affects what part of the operating system.

The guide is in very simple and easy-to-understand language and is deliberately written in this way to let everyone get the most out of it.

As a reader your feedback will help a great deal in improving future books by the author. As per the feedback future improvements may include:

- •^: More simplified language for non-technical home users and corporate employees.
- •^: Technically rich contents for IT professionals.
- •^: More Real World Scenario Tips with more complex and practical examples.
- •^: More screen shots for better understanding.

Readers can send their feedbacks to: **vivek.nayyar1107@gmail.com**

MANAGING MICROSOFT WINDOWS 7 TRHOUGH GROUP POLICIES

Introduction to Group Policies

Group Policies are the advanced configuration options offered by Microsoft operating systems that allow users to modify the settings of the OS more granularly. In almost all cases, modifications done in Group Policies directly modify registry settings of the Windows and therefore it is strongly recommended that the Group Policies must be handled by technically qualified professionals only. This is the reason why the Group Policies are not available as any menu or window in Microsoft Windows operating systems and administrators must open the Group Policies console before they can make any changes to them.

Group Polices and Group Policy Objects

Group Policies contain multiple options and each option can be double clicked to make appropriate changes to it. These options are mostly referred to as Group Policy Objects (GPOs). GPOs, when initialized are opened in their respective consoles, normally known as snap-ins. In order to access GPOs in Microsoft Windows 7, Microsoft Management Console (MMC) must be initialized by typing MMC command in the Search box that is available at the bottom of start menu or in the Run command box. Once initialized multiple snap-ins can be added to the console and can be managed simultaneously. Alternatively, administrators can also type GPEDIT.MSC command and press Enter key in order to initiate and access Local Computer Policy snap-in directly. Local Computer Policy snap-in allows administrators to configure almost every setting that an administrator may need to secure and customize a local computer.

Credentials Required for Group Policy Management

Under normal circumstances and by default only the accounts that belong to Administrators group are allowed to access and manage Group Policies in every Microsoft-based operating system. Any user that belongs to non-Administrators group cannot modify the Group Policy settings whatsoever.

In all, Group Policy settings allow administrators of computers to customize the operating systems granularly which is not possible through Control Panel or any other configuration option.

Rename Local Built-in Administrator Account

When Windows 7 is installed an administrator account is automatically created and by default it is disabled. This is due to security reasons so that no one can misuse the unrestricted privileges of the account. In many production environments, however, to make the network even securer administrators rename the default name, which is Administrator, of built-in administrator account. The reason behind this is just to double up the security and make it harder for hackers to guess the username and the password. If administrator account is not renamed, hackers only have to guess the password as they already know that default account name is always Administrator. As an administrator you can rename the built-in Administrator account by going to **Computer Management> Local Users and Groups> Users**. This method will rename the default Administrator account on a single computer. However in domain environments group policies can be used for these tasks, which work in more efficient manner. Therefore if you want to rename Administrator account through group policy you need to follow the steps given below:

1. Log on to the computer with administrator account.
2. Click **Start** button.
3. At bottom of start menu in search box type **GPEDIT.MSC** command and press enter key.
4. On **Local Group Policy Editor** snap-in under **Computer Configuration** expand **Windows Settings** and then expand **Security Settings**.
5. Expand **Local Policies** and click **Security Options**.

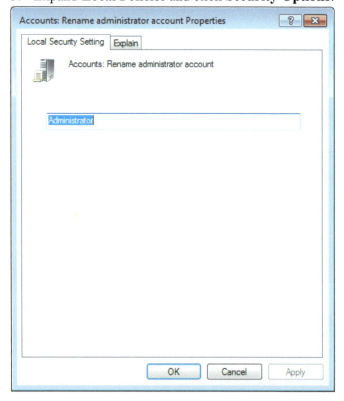

6. From the right pane double click **Accounts: Rename administrator** and on the opened box type a new name for the administrator account.

7. Once done, click **Ok** button and close **Local Group Policy Editor** snap-in.

8. Open **Command Prompt** and in command window type **GPUPDATE /FORCE** to update here computer policy with latest configuration.

9. Close **Command Prompt**.

Define Maximum Age of User Account Password

Base of security in any platform, including Microsoft Windows 7, is passwords and therefore they should be kept with utmost care and precaution. Also, it is always recommended that passwords must be changed on a regular basis in order to protect any hacker from guessing them. In complex network set-ups where users are not allowed to change their passwords, Windows 7 provides a group policy setting using which administrators can define a lifespan of passwords after which the operating system prompts users to change it. Users are then enforced to change their passwords failing to which they cannot log on to the computer whatsoever. As an administrator you can specify the maximum password age by following the steps given below:

1. Log on to the computer with administrator account.

2. Click **Start** button.

3. At the bottom of start menu in search box type **GPEDIT.MSC** command and press enter key.

4. On **Local Group Policy Editor** snap-in under **Computer Configuration** expand **Windows Settings** and then expand **Security Settings**.

5. From the opened list expand **Account Policies** and from the list click **Password Policies**.

6. From the right pane double click **Maximum password age** and from the opened window in **Password expires in** box specify the number of days after which the passwords will expire and Windows will prompt users to change them.

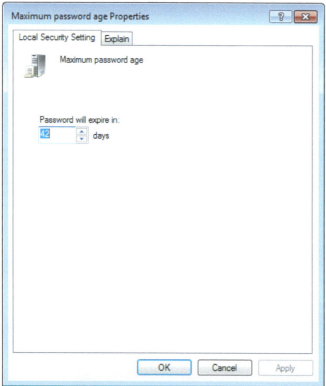

7. Once done, click **Ok** button to accept and confirm your configuration and close **Local Group Policy Editor** snap-in.

8. Open **Command Prompt** and in command window type **GPUPDATE /FORCE** to update here computer policy with latest configuration.

9. Close **Command Prompt**.

More Info:

Default password age is 42 days.

When this setting is applied user are allowed to change passwords.

Specify Minimum Password Length

In medium or large scale industries where there are complex network scenarios administrators may want to specify the minimum character length of user account passwords in order to make the network setups even securer. This type of configuration can easily be seen by creating a new user account on any publicly available email service providing sites. Examples can include Gmail, Yahoo mail, etc. While registering for these services minimum password character length is 6 and sometimes 8. In the same way administrators can define minimum password length of user accounts on a Windows 7 computer by following the steps given below:

1. Log on to the computer with administrator account.

2. Click **Start** button.

3. At bottom of start menu in search box type **GPEDIT.MSC** command and press enter key.

4. On **Local Group Policy Editor** snap-in under **Computer Configuration** expand **Windows Settings** and then expand **Security Settings**.

5. From the opened list expand **Account Policies** and from the list click **Password Policies**.

6. From the right pane double click **Minimum password length** and from **Minimum password length Properties** box in **Password must be at least** textbox specify the minimum length of password in numbers.

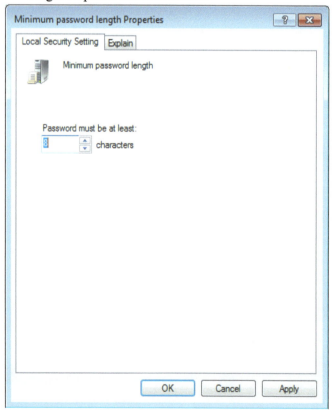

7. Once done, click **Ok** button to accept and confirm your configuration and close **Local Group Policy Editor** snap-in.

8. Open **Command Prompt** and in command window type **GPUPDATE /FORCE** to update here computer policy with latest configuration.

9. Close **Command Prompt**.

Delete Inactive User Profiles Automatically

By default Windows 7 projects every data that is stored on the computer. This includes user profiles as well. However in the cases where many users share a common PC it is always advisable to delete inactive user profiles on a regular basis in order to save disk space and avoid the chances of system getting overpopulated with junk data. With the help of group policies administrators can define a threshold time after which an inactive user profile will automatically be deleted. For example if an administrator has defined the threshold period of 30 days, in this case if a user fails to logon within the specified time his profile will be deleted automatically. As an administrator you can configure this setting by following the steps given below:

1. Log on to the computer with administrator account.
2. Click **Start** button.
3. At the bottom of start menu in search box type **GPEDIT.MSC** and press enter key.
4. On **Local Group Policy Editor** snap-in under **Computer Configuration** expand **Administrative Templates** and expand **System**.
5. From the list click **User Profiles** and from the right pane double click **Delete user profiles older than a specified number of days on system restart**..

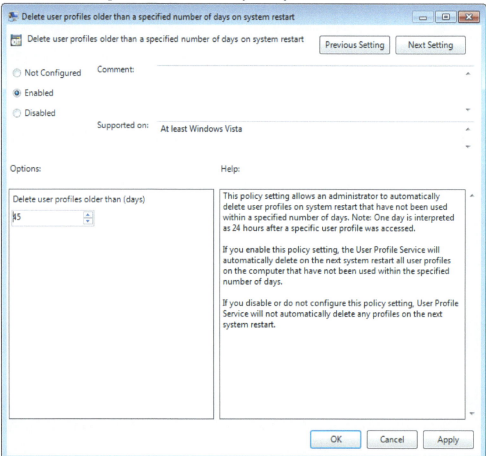

6. On the opened box select **Enabled** radio button and in the **Options** pane specify the number of days after which you want the inactive user profile to get deleted automatically.

7. Once done, click **Ok** button to accept and confirm your configuration and close **Local Group Policy Editor** snap-in.

8. Open **Command Prompt** and the command window type **GPUPDATE /FORCE** to update your computer with latest settings.

9. Close **Command Prompt**.

Modifying User Account Control (UAC) Settings

Many people think that User Account Control or UAC is not mandatory and is quite annoying when a user needs to perform some administrative tasks. In terms of security, however, this is not true. User Account Control is a feature which was introduced in Windows Vista and now it is carried forward to Windows 7 and Windows Server 2008. Because of User Account Control your computer remains safe from harmful virus attacks. Also Windows 7 computer is protected from malicious scripts which are written by destructive users in order to harm the computers of other users.

User Account Control has two types of prompts which are initiated as per the credentials used to log on to the computer. This means that if a user is logged on with an administrative credential he will receive Prompt for Consent. In

this prompt, user needs not to provide password if he wants to perform any administrative tasks. Instead he just needs to click Yes button to allow Windows 7 to continue. On the other hand if a user is logged on to the Windows 7 computer with user credentials or limited access he will be presented with Prompt for Credentials box in which the user has to provide administrator's password in order to perform any administrative task.

You can add an extra layer of security by configuring Windows 7 to prompt for credentials even when a user is logged on with administrator account. To do this you need to follow the instructions given below:

1. Click on **Start** button.
2. At the bottom of start menu in search box type **GPEDIT.MSC**.
3. In the **Local Computer Policy** snap-in under **Computer Configuration** expand **Windows Settings**.
4. Expand **Security Settings**.
5. Expand **Local Policies**.
6. Select **Security Options**.
7. In the right pane double click on **User Account Control: Behavior off the elevation prompt for administrators in Admin Approval Mode**.
8. In the opened window from the drop-down list select **Prompt for Credentials**.
9. Click **Ok** button to accept and confirm your selection.
10. Close **Local Computer Policy** snap-in.
11. Click **Start** button and go to **All Programs**.
12. From the list select Accessories.
13. Right-click **Command Prompt** and select **Run as Administrator**.

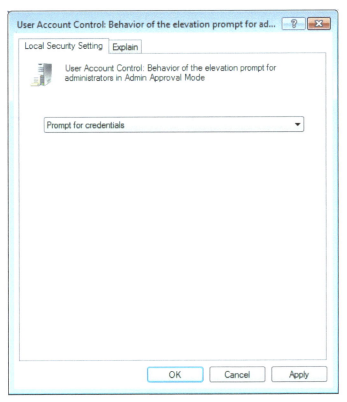

14. In the **User Account Control** dialog box click **Ok** button to allow Windows to use your administrative credentials to run the program.

15. In the **Administrator: Command Prompt** window type **GPUPDATE /FORCE** and press enter key.

With the help of this method any malicious script will not be able to run because it will ask for the password every time administrative privileges are required. This setting also ensures that if an administrator of Windows 7 computer wants to install any application, it is a willful activity and the task is intentionally initiated.

Make Password Mandatory for All User Accounts

As you might have seen in almost all account registration processes, providing password is mandatory and without which an account cannot be created. Although any user account that is created can remain without password, however this feature can be modified and the computer can be configured to enforce users and administrators to provide passwords. Moreover the computer can also be configured so that the password that a user provides must also be a complex password. Because of this configuration users cannot provide a simple password and/or cannot leave the passwords blank.

To make this happen you need to follow the below steps:

1. Click **Start** button.
2. At the bottom of the list in the **Search Box** type **GPEDIT.MSC** and press enter key.
3. From the **Local Computer Policy** snap-in under **Computer Configuration** expand **Windows Settings**.
4. From **Windows Settings** tree, expand **Security Setting**.
5. Then expand **Account Policies** and select **Password Policies**.
6. From the right pane double-click **Password Must Meet Complexity Requirements**.
7. On **Password Must Meet Complexity Requirements Properties** page select **Enabled**.

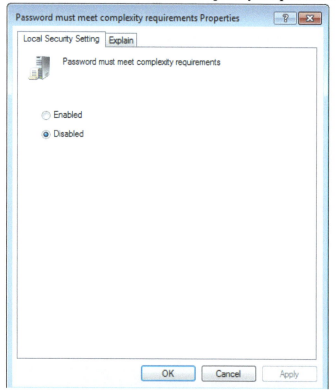

8. Press **Ok** button on all the vendors to accept and confirm your selections.

Create a new user account and try to leave the password field blank while creating. You will get an error message telling that your password does not meet requirements.

Guidelines for a complex password:

Complex password means that a password must have minimum of 7 characters having the combination of any three of the following four options:

1. Special characters. For example: !, @, #, $, %, ^
2. Characters with upper cases. For example: A, R, G, S, R, E
3. Characters with lower cases. For example: a, g, w, t, e
4. Numerical digits. For example: 123456

An example for a complex password can be: c0mP1@x

Restrict Users from Repeating Same Passwords

In complex network setups administrators define maximum password age in order to make the setup even securer. This configuration enforces users to keep on changing their passwords on regular basis. Sometimes, however, users get annoyed and frustrated by these prompts as they appear on their screens every now and then and they may type the same password every time the operating system prompts for a change. Administrators can restrict users from doing so by following the steps given below:

1. Log on to the computer with administrator account.

2. Click **Start** button.

3. At the bottom of start menu in search box type **GPEDIT.MSC** command and press enter key.

4. On **Local Group Policy Editor** snap-in under **Computer Configuration** expand **Windows Settings** and then expand **Security Settings**.

5. From the opened list expand **Account Policies** and from the list click **Password Policies**.

6. From the right pane double click **Enforce password history** and from the opened window in editable box specify the number of passwords that Windows 7 must remember. (For example, if you specify 3, in this case windows will not allow users to use the same password till next 3 password expirations)

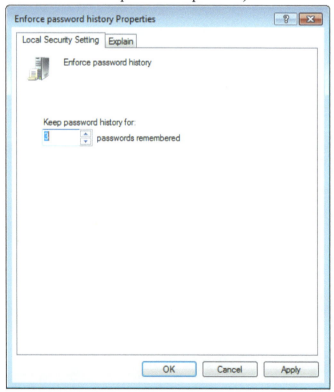

7. Click **Ok** button to accept and confirm your configuration and close **Local Group Policy Editor** snap-in.

8. Open **Command Prompt** and in command window type **GPUPDATE /FORCE** to update here computer policy with latest configuration.

9. Close **Command Prompt**.

Set Minimum Password Age

When Maximum Password Age group policy setting is configured users are automatically allowed to change their passwords after the specified period of time. However due to security reasons administrators may not want users to change their passwords before a certain amount of time. As an administrator you can restrict users from changing their passwords before specified time by defining Minimum Password Age which can be configured by following the steps given below:

1. Log on to the computer with administrator account.
2. Click **Start** button.
3. At bottom of start menu in search box type **GPEDIT.MSC** command and press enter key.
4. On **Local Group Policy Editor** snap-in under **Computer Configuration** expand **Windows Settings** and then expand **Security Settings**.
5. From the opened list expand **Account Policies** and from the list click **Password Policies**.
6. From the right pane double click **Minimum password age** and from the opened window in **Password can be changed immediately after** box specify the number of days before which users will not be able to change passwords.

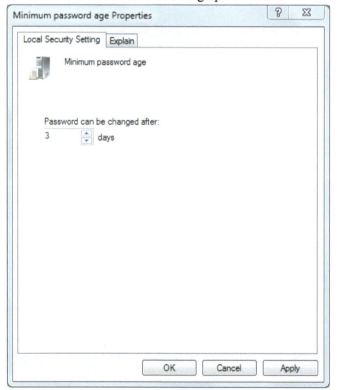

7. Once done, click **Ok** button to accept and confirm your configuration and close **Local Group Policy Editor** snap-in.

8. Open **Command Prompt** and in command window type **GPUPDATE /FORCE** to update here computer policy with latest configuration.

9. Close **Command Prompt**.

Enforce Users to Press Ctrl+Alt+Del before Logging

Feature of pressing Ctrl+Alt+Del is by default enabled on any network operating system, that is, Windows Server 2003 and Windows Server 2008. Also, when a client computer is added to a domain it inherits this feature and enforces domain users to press this key combination before they get logon dialog box. However if administrators want, they can configure this setting on a Windows 7 computer which is either in a workgroup environment or is not connected to any network at all. This setting although adds an extra layer of security, it is not recommended on home computers in order to make things easier for home users. As an administrator if you want to configure this you can follow the steps given below:

1. Log on to the computer with administrator account.

2. Click **Start** button.

3. At bottom of start menu in search box type **GPEDIT.MSC** command and press enter key.

4. On **Local Group Policy Editor** snap-in under **Computer Configuration** expand **Windows Settings** and then expand **Security Settings**.

5. Expand **Local Policies** and click **Security Options**.

6. From the right pane double click **Interactive logon: Do not require CTRL+ALT+DEL** and on the opened Window select **Enabled** radio button.

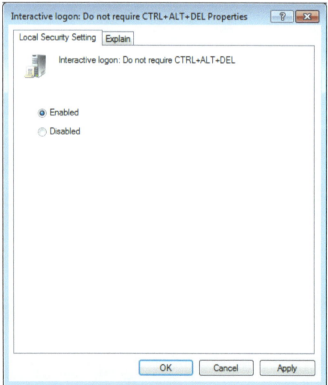

7. Once done, click **Ok** button and close **Local Group Policy Editor** snap-in.

8. Open **Command Prompt** and in command window type **GPUPDATE /FORCE** to update here computer policy with latest configuration.

9. Close **Command Prompt**.

Locking User Accounts after Invalid Logons

There are times when users forget their passwords and they keep on attempting logging on using wrong passwords. By default Windows 7 allows users to retry logging on to the computer unlimited number of times. In home environment this default configuration is ideal and doesn't require any modifications. However, in production environment this may offer promising advantages to hackers and they can continue trying invalid logon attempts till they get success. As an administrator you can limit the number of invalid logon attempts by following the steps given below:

1. Log on to the computer with administrator account.

2. Click **Start** button.

3. At bottom of start menu in search box type **GPEDIT.MSC** command and press enter key.

4. On **Local Group Policy Editor** snap-in under **Computer Configuration** expand **Windows Settings** and then expand **Security Settings**.

5. From the opened list expand **Account Policies** and from the list click **Account Lockout Policy** and from the right pane double click **Account lockout threshold**.

6. On **Account lockout threshold Properties** box in the editable textbox specify the number of invalid logon attempts after which that particular account with be locked and click **Ok** button. Alternatively, you can change

7. On **Suggested Value Changes** box accept the default configuration by clicking **Ok** button and close **Local Group Policy Editor** snap-in.

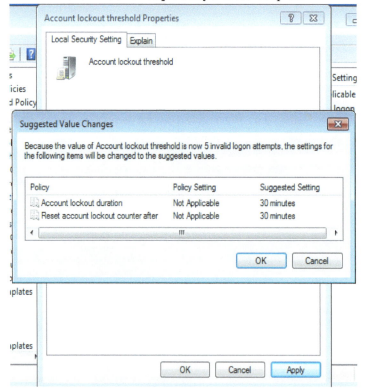

8. Open **Command Prompt** and in command window type **GPUPDATE /FORCE** to update here computer policy with latest configuration.

9. Close **Command Prompt**.

Do Not Display Last Logged on User Name

By default on Windows logon screen Windows 7 displays the name of the most recent logged on user. For home environments this setup is not a major issue as it is always assumed that in homes no hackers are present. However, in medium or large-scale industries where there are several users administrators may not want any user to know which user logged on to the machine before him. Administrators may want to configure this setting for security reasons and as an administrator if you want to configure this you need to follow the steps given below:

1. Log on to the computer with administrator account.

2. Click **Start** button.

3. At bottom of start menu in search box type **GPEDIT.MSC** command and press enter key.

4. On **Local Group Policy Editor** snap-in under **Computer Configuration** expand **Windows Settings** and then expand **Security Settings**.

5. Expand **Local Policies** and click **Security Options**.

6. From the right pane double click on **Interactive logon: Do not display last user name** and on the opened box select **Enabled** radio button.

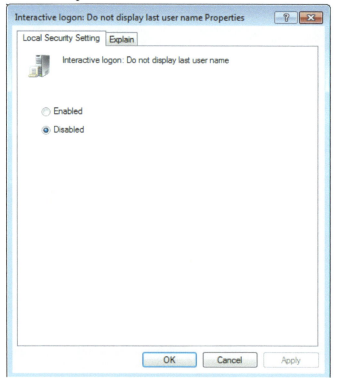

7. Once done, click **Ok** button and close **Local Group Policy Editor** snap-in.

8. Open **Command Prompt** and in command window type **GPUPDATE /FORCE** to update here computer policy with latest configuration.

9. Close **Command Prompt**.

Specify Maximum Password Age for Domain Clients

When a Windows 7 computer is added to a domain its computer account is automatically created and is registered with the domain controller. Whenever a domain user attempts to log on to the domain using any client computer first of all Windows 7 computer account password is authenticated with the domain controller and once the authentication is successful, user account and password is authenticated with active directory database. Just like user accounts, computer accounts also have password expiration dates after which domain controllers do now allow users to use that computer to log on to the domain. However computer account passwords are renewed automatically. As an administrator you can increase or decrease the maximum password age of computer accounts when they are member of a domain by following the steps given below:

1. Log on to the computer with administrator account.

2. Click **Start** button.

3. At bottom of start menu in search box type **GPEDIT.MSC** command and press enter key.

4. On **Local Group Policy Editor** snap-in under **Computer Configuration** expand **Windows Settings** and then expand **Security Settings**.

5. Expand **Local Policies** and click **Security Options**.

6. From the right pane double click **Domain member: Maximum machine account password age** and on the opened Window in available box specify the maximum password age of machine account.

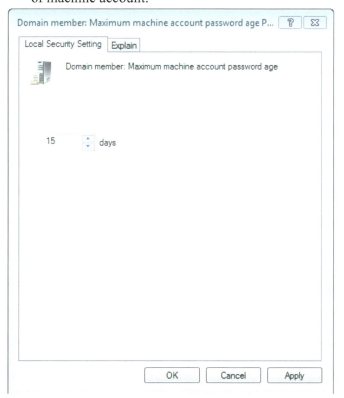

7. Once done, click **Ok** button and close **Local Group Policy Editor** snap-in.

8. Open **Command Prompt** and in command window type **GPUPDATE /FORCE** to update here computer policy with latest configuration.

9. Close **Command Prompt**.

Notifications Password Change before Expiration

Whenever Windows is left with default configuration passwords for user accounts expire after 42 days and users start receiving the notifications 14 days prior password expiration. This configuration is default and generally should not be modified. However in some complex network scenarios where security is considered major issue administrators may want to modify this configuration in order to notify users about the expiration date. As an administrator you can configure this setting by following the steps given below:

1. Log on to the computer with administrator account.

2. Click **Start** button.

3. At bottom of start menu in search box type **GPEDIT.MSC** command and press enter key.

4. On **Local Group Policy Editor** snap-in under **Computer Configuration** expand **Windows Settings** and then expand **Security Settings**.

5. Expand **Local Policies** and click **Security Options**.

6. From the right pane double click **Interactive logon: Prompt user to change password before expiration** and on the opened Window in **Begin prompting this many days before password expires** box specify the duration you want users to start receiving notifications before expiration.

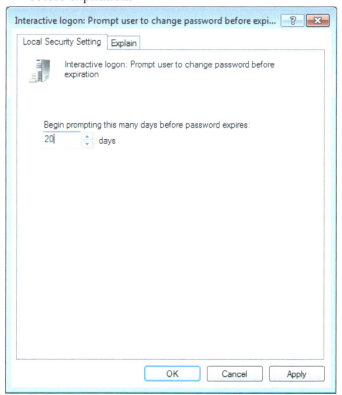

7. Once done, click **Ok** button and close **Local Group Policy Editor** snap-in.

8. Open **Command Prompt** and in command window type **GPUPDATE /FORCE** to update here computer policy with latest configuration.

9. Close **Command Prompt**.

Enable Object Access Audit Policy

As everyone knows no security plan is foolproof. However possibilities of security breaches can be reduced considerably by proper and regular monitoring of your computer systems and/or entire network setup. Auditing plays an important role when dealing with security and monitoring. With the help of auditing you can keep a close eye on every event that takes place in your network infrastructure. Though there are several auditing policies that can be configured on a Windows 7 computer, but when talking about objects and resources you need to enable Object Access audit policy to monitor a particular object. By enabling object access audit policy you can monitor which user or group tried to access the object. If you want to enable Object Access Audit Policy on your Windows 7 computer you need to follow the steps given below:

1. Log on to your Windows 7 computer with the administrator account as the policies can only be configured with administrator privileges.

2. Go to start menu and in the search box type **GPEDIT.MSC**.

3. On the opened snap-in under **Computer Configuration** expand **Windows Settings** and then expand **Security Settings**.

4. From the expanded tree expand **Local Policies** and click **Audit Policy**.

5. From the right pane double click **Audit object access** and from the opened **Properties** box check both **Success** and **Failure** checkboxes.

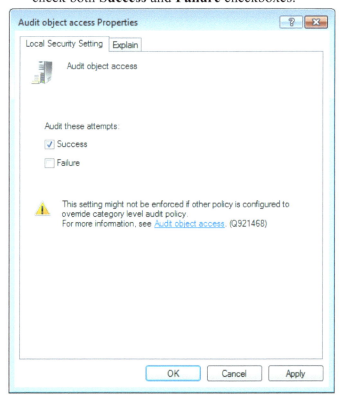

6. Click **Ok** button to accept your configuration and finally close **Local Group Policy Editor** snap-in.

7. In order to make the configuration take effect you need to run **GPUPDATE /FORCE** command in the **Command Prompt**.

Note: Enabling object access from the group policies alone will not solve the purpose. In order to make object access policy fully functional you need to enable auditing on the object you want to monitor. Also you need to specify the user account or the group for which you want to apply the auditing on that particular object.

Enable Logon Events Audit Policy

Normally it is not possible to know who used your computer when you were not present. The only thing that Windows 7 offers, under normal settings, is to view the name of the user who recently logged on. In home environments this configuration is quite ideal and even if home users are not able to see the recently logged on user name it hardly matters to them. However in production environments where security is a major concern administrators would definitely want to know who used which computer and when? To solve the purpose, Microsoft offers a promising audit feature using which you can monitor a computer and can find who used the computer and at what time? You can enable Audit Logon Event audit policy to track logon events on your computer and to do so you need to follow the steps given below:

1. Log on to your Windows 7 computer with any account that is a member of Administrators group.

2. Go to start menu and in the search box type **GPEDIT.MSC** command and press enter.

3. In the snap-in under **Computer Configuration** expand **Windows Settings** and then expand **Security Settings**.

4. Expand **Local Policies** and click **Audit Policy**.

5. In the right pane double click **Audit logon events** and from the opened **Properties** box check both **Success** and **Failure** checkboxes to enable logon event logging.

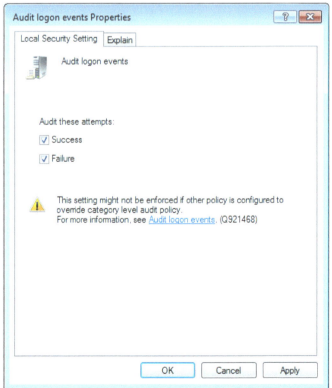

6. Click **Ok** button to accept the settings.

7. Use Command Prompt to update your computer with the latest configuration by typing **GPUPDATE /FORCE** command in it.

Biometrics Authentication for Domain Users

As default configuration Windows 7 allows only local users to authenticate using biometric devices. In home environments or in small-scale industries where computers are connected in a workgroup this configuration is quite ideal and should not be modified. However when working with medium or large scale industries where there are several computers connected to a domain and users mostly work on domain accounts, Windows 7 computers should be allowed to accept biometric authentication for domain users for easier logon process. As an administrator you can configure this by following the steps given below:

1. Log on to the computer with administrator account.
2. Click **Start** button.
3. At the bottom of start menu in search box type **GPEDIT.MSC** and press enter key.
4. On **Local Group Policy Editor** snap-in under **Computer Configuration** expand **Administrative Templates** and expand **Windows Components**.
5. From the expanded list click **Biometrics** and from the right pane double click **Allow domain users to log on using biometrics**.
6. On the opened window select **Disabled** radio button and click **Ok** button to accept and confirm your configuration.

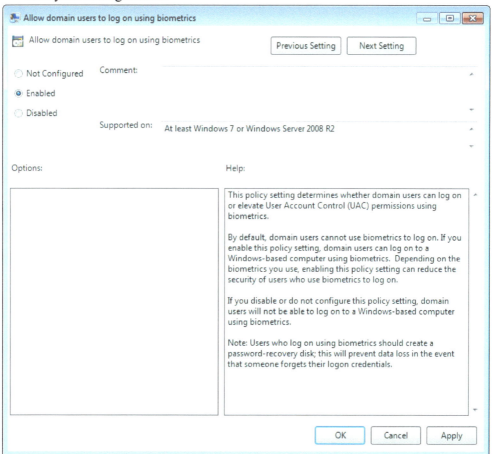

7. Close **Local Group Policy Editor** snap-in and open **Command Prompt**.

8. In command window type **GPUPDATE /FORCE** and press enter key to update your computer configuration with latest settings.

9. Close **Command Prompt**.

Deny Log on Using Biometric Authentication

In computers where biometric sensor devices are available users can log on by providing their biometric identification. Users can also elevate User Account Control permissions using biometric authentications. Since biometric authentication is considered genuine and authentic it is by default enabled when Windows 7 is installed on a computer. However in some cases or in some machines where no biometric sensor devices are available administrators may want to disable this feature in order to protect the computers from hackers' attacks. If you are an administrator you can disable biometric authentication to log on or to elevate User Account Control by following the steps given below:

1. Log on to the computer with administrator account.
2. Click **Start** button.
3. At the bottom of start menu in search box type **GPEDIT.MSC** and press enter key.
4. On **Local Group Policy Editor** snap-in under **Computer Configuration** expand **Administrative Templates** and expand **Windows Components**.
5. From the expanded list click **Biometrics** and from the right pane double click **Allow users to log on using biometrics**.
6. On the opened window select **Disabled** radio button and click **Ok** button to accept and confirm your configuration.

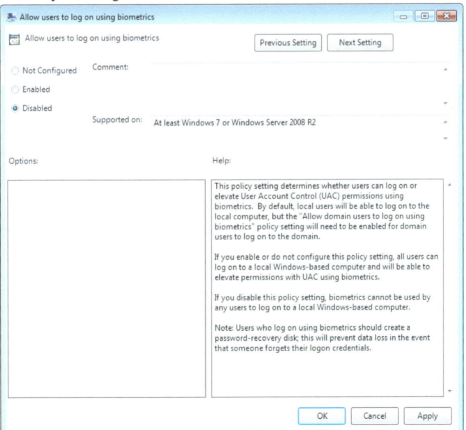

7. Close **Local Group Policy Editor** snap-in and open **Command Prompt**.

8. In command window type **GPUPDATE /FORCE** and press enter key to update your computer configuration with latest settings.

9. Close **Command Prompt**.

Display Text Message When Users' Logon Attempts

For legal purposes many times administrators of almost every network may want to notify users about the policies of the organization they work with. These policies may include assurance of utmost secrecy of sensitive data, misuse of any office equipment, etc. When this is the case administrators can configure Windows 7 computer to notify users every time they logon reminding them about the policies. For home users this option might be useful as a reminder of any To Do task. As an administrator you can configure this setting by following the steps given below:

1. Log on to the computer with administrator account.
2. Click **Start** button.
3. At bottom of start menu in search box type **GPEDIT.MSC** command and press enter key.
4. On **Local Group Policy Editor** snap-in under **Computer Configuration** expand **Windows Settings** and then expand **Security Settings**.
5. Expand **Local Policies** and click **Security Options**.
6. From the right pane double click **Interactive logon: Message text for users attempting to logon** and on the opened Window type your message in the available text box and click **Ok** button.
7. Double click **Interactive logon: Message title for users attempting to logon** and on the opened Window in available text box type the title of the message box that will be displayed to the users. (For example: Warning!!).
8. Once done, click **Ok** button and close **Local Group Policy Editor** snap-in.
9. Open **Command Prompt** and in command window type **GPUPDATE /FORCE** to update here computer policy with latest configuration.
10. Close **Command Prompt**.

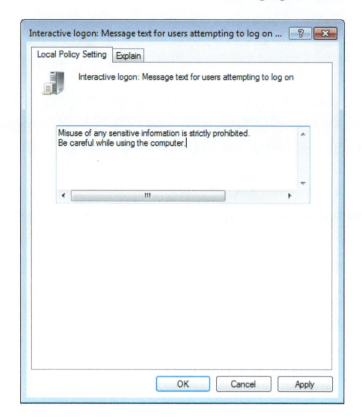

Enforce Users to Logon before Shutting Down

When a computer starts users can log on using their credentials. In some cases it might be possible that as soon as the users start their computers they need to go out for some reasons and because of which they need to shut down the computers instantaneously. By default Windows 7 allows users to shut down their computers even when they are not logged on, i.e. right from the welcome screen. Assuming that Windows 7 is client operating system and is mostly used in home environments this configuration is enabled by default. However when Windows 7 computer is used in complex network scenarios, that is in production environments, it is recommended that administrators should disable this feature so that users cannot shut down the computers without logging on to them. Moreover, in some cases administrators disable the shutdown feature as well. If you want to enforce users to log on to a Windows 7 computer in order to shut it down you need to follow the steps given below:

1. Log on to the computer with administrator account.

2. Click **Start** button.

3. At bottom of start menu in search box type **GPEDIT.MSC** command and press enter key.

4. On **Local Group Policy Editor** snap-in under **Computer Configuration** expand **Windows Settings** and then expand **Security Settings**.

5. Expand **Local Policies** and click **Security Options**.

6. From the right pane double click **Shutdown: Allow system to be shut down without having to log on** and on the opened box select **Disabled** radio button.

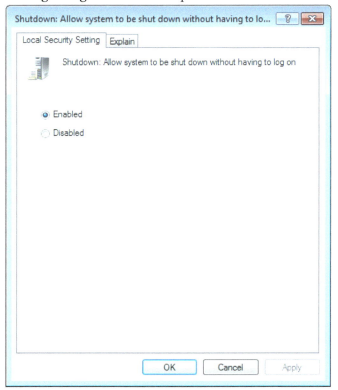

7. Once done, click **Ok** button and close **Local Group Policy Editor** snap-in.

8. Open **Command Prompt** and in command window type **GPUPDATE /FORCE** to update here computer policy with latest configuration.

9. Close **Command Prompt**.

Locally Cached Domain Logon Information Count

When a Windows 7 computer is joined to a domain, domain users get authenticated from the domain controller. As a domain user types his/her username and password on any client computer and chooses domain authentication method, his credentials are sent to the domain controller for authentication. Sometimes domain controllers might not be available because of any reason. When this is the case domain users are not able to contact domain controllers for authentication and thus Windows 7 allows them to log on to the computer using domain user's cached credentials that automatically gets cached on the local system. By default Windows 7 computer caches up to 10 logons, however administrators can modify and increase or decrease this number by following the steps given below:

1. Log on to the computer with administrator account.

2. Click **Start** button.

3. At bottom of start menu in search box type **GPEDIT.MSC** command and press enter key.

4. On **Local Group Policy Editor** snap-in under **Computer Configuration** expand **Windows Settings** and then expand **Security Settings**.

5. Expand **Local Policies** and click **Security Options**.

6. From the right pane double click **Interactive logon: Number of previous logons to cache (in case Domain Controller is not available)** and on the opened Window in **Cache** box specify the number of logons which you want Windows 7 computer to cache.

7. Once done, click **Ok** button and close **Local Group Policy Editor** snap-in.

8. Open **Command Prompt** and in command window type **GPUPDATE /FORCE** to update here computer policy with latest configuration.

9. Close **Command Prompt**.

Terminate Domain Session after Logon Time Ends

In complex domain/client network setups users mostly authenticate their credentials from domain controllers. If administrators in these cases have made the network even securer by assigning specific log on hours for domain users, users cannot log on to the domain at unspecified log on hours . However in the cases when users are logged on to the domain and during that period their logon hours expire they are not automatically disconnected from the sessions. In the organizations where security is considered major issue this default configuration might cause potential risks to the entire domain environment. If you are an administrator in any such organization you can disable this feature and enforce disconnection of logged on user accounts as soon as their logon hours expire by following the steps given below:

1. Log on to the computer with administrator account.
2. Click **Start** button.
3. At bottom of start menu in search box type **GPEDIT.MSC** command and press enter key.
4. On **Local Group Policy Editor** snap-in under **Computer Configuration** expand **Windows Settings** and then expand **Security Settings**.
5. Expand **Local Policies** and click on **Security Options**.
6. From the right pane double click **Network security: Force logoff when logon hours expire** and on the opened box select **Enabled** radio button.

7. Once done, click **Ok** button and close **Local Group Policy Editor** snap-in.

8. Open **Command Prompt** and in command window type **GPUPDATE /FORCE** to update here computer policy with latest configuration.

9. Close **Command Prompt**.

Note: This configuration is only effective when used in domain environments this policy is configured in Default Domain Policy GPO.

Make Entire Folder Tree Available Offline

When Windows 7 is installed and is in its default configuration, it always asks users to make sub-folders available offline whenever they try to configure offline availability of any parent folder. This allows users to choose appropriate option as per their requirements. However in some cases administrators or home users may want to make entire folder tree available offline by default, that is, every time any folder is configured to become available offline. As an administrator you can configure Windows group policy settings to do so by following the steps given below:

1. Log on to the computer with administrator account.
2. Click **Start** button.
3. At the bottom of start menu in search box type **GPEDIT.MSC** and press enter key.
4. On **Local Group Policy Editor** snap-in under **Computer Configuration** expand **Administrative Templates** and expand **Network**.
5. From the expanded list click **Offline Files** and from the right pane double click **Subfolders always available offline**.
6. On the opened box select **Enabled** radio button and click **Ok** button to accept and confirm your configuration.

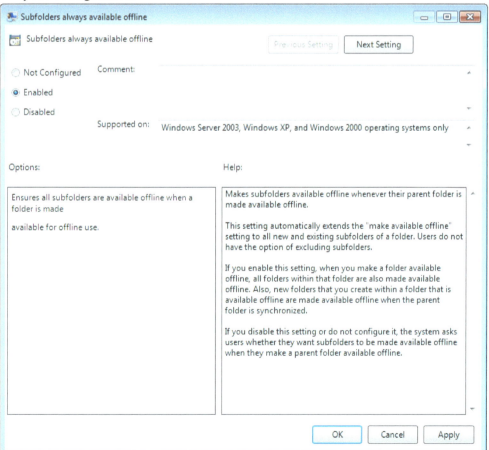

7. Once done, close **Local Group Policy Editor** snap-in and open **Command Prompt.**

8. In the command window type **GPUPDATE /FORCE** to update your computer with latest settings.

9. Close **Command Prompt**.

Make Some Files Always Available Offline

In any production environment when a Windows 7 computer is connected to a network, administrators may want to make some files or folders always available offline to the users who need access to them on regular basis. This can easily be done through group policy settings and administrative privileges are required to do so. When a Windows 7 computer is connected to a workgroup environment (more likely in a small-scale industry or Small Office/Home Office), administrators can configure this setting on individual computers by following the steps given below:

1. Log on to the computer with administrator account.
2. Click **Start** button.
3. At the bottom of start menu in search box type **GPEDIT.MSC** and press enter key.
4. On **Local Group Policy Editor** snap-in under **Computer Configuration** expand **Administrative Templates** and expand **Network**.
5. From the expanded list click **Offline Files** and from the right pane double click **Administratively assigned offline files**.
6. On the opened box select **Enabled** radio button and in the **Options** section click **Show** button.

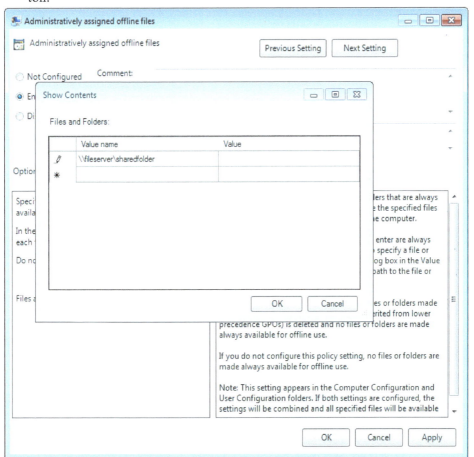

7. On **Show Contents** box type the UNC shared path of the files and/or folder you want to make available offline administratively under **Value name** column and click **Ok** button to accept and confirm your configuration.

8. Once done, close **Local Group Policy Editor** snap-in and open **Command Prompt.**

9. In the command window type **GPUPDATE /FORCE** to update your computer with latest settings.

10. Close **Command Prompt**.

Offline Files Synchronization at Users' Logon

In Windows 7 you can manage the time when the cached copies of offline files stored on the local computer will be synchronized with the original copies stored at the file server. This can be managed through group policies. In some cases administrators may want to enable offline file synchronization as soon as a user logs on to the Windows 7 computer. This is to ensure that whenever a user is connected to the network he gets the latest and updated versions of files. As an administrator of a Windows 7 computer you can configure this by following the steps given below:

1. Log on to the computer with administrator account.

2. Click **Start** button.

3. At the bottom of start menu in search box type **GPEDIT.MSC** and press enter key.

4. On **Local Group Policy Editor** snap-in under **Computer Configuration** expand **Administrative Templates** and expand **Network**.

5. From the expanded list click **Offline Files** and from the right pane double click **Synchronize all offline files when logging on**.

6. On the opened box select **Enabled** radio button and click **Ok** button to accept and confirm your configuration.

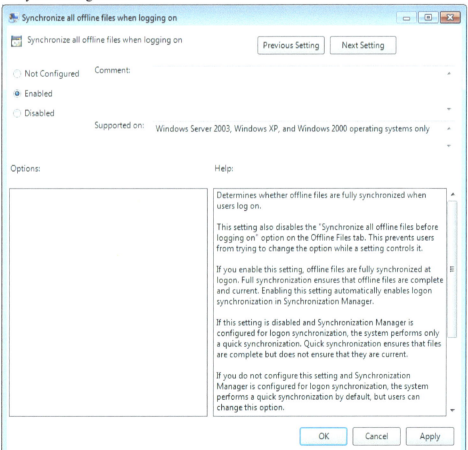

7. Once done, close **Local Group Policy Editor** snap-in and open **Command Prompt.**

8. In the command window type **GPUPDATE /FORCE** to update your computer with latest settings.

9. Close **Command Prompt**.

Synchronize Offline Files at Users Logoff

When users are connected to the file server, this means that they are working on the files which are located on remote computers. Some companies allow users to take their personal files offline (store a cached copy of the files on their local computers) so that they can work on them even if the file server is not available because of any reason. When this is the case offline file synchronization becomes an essential part in order to keep users updated with latest versions of the files. With the help of group policy settings in Windows 7 administrators can now configure the computers to synchronize cached copies of offline files on the local computers with the files stored on the file servers before users log off. As an administrator you can configure this by following the steps given below:

1. Log on to the computer with administrator account.
2. Click **Start** button.
3. At the bottom of start menu in search box type **GPEDIT.MSC** and press enter key.
4. On **Local Group Policy Editor** snap-in under **Computer Configuration** expand **Administrative Templates** and expand **Network**.
5. From the expanded list click **Offline Files** and from the right pane double click **Synchronize all offline files before logging off**.

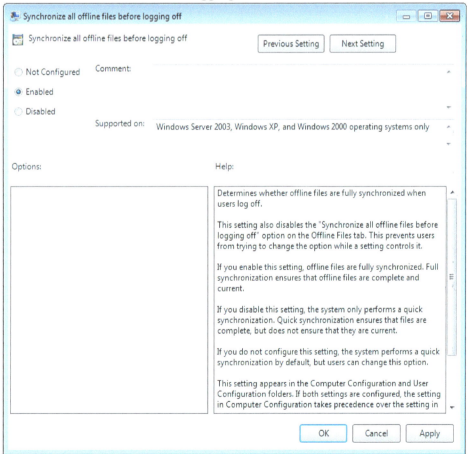

6. On the opened box select **Enabled** radio button and click **Ok** button to accept and confirm your configuration.

7. Once done, close **Local Group Policy Editor** snap-in and open **Command Prompt.**

8. In the command window type **GPUPDATE /FORCE** to update your computer with latest settings.

9. Close **Command Prompt**.

Manage Offline Files When Windows is Suspended

There are times when users work with offline files which are locally cached on their computers. These offline files are the cached copies of files which are actually stored on some remote computer (file server). These files are made available offline so that users can work on them even if the file server goes down. Also, by default Windows 7 computers go to either hibernation or sleep mode when users fail to interact with them for specific time duration. When this is the case you can manage the nature of offline file synchronization through group policies so that they can synchronize completely to provide users latest versions of offline files. You can do this by following the steps given below:

1. Log on to the computer with administrator account.
2. Click **Start** button.
3. At the bottom of start menu in search box type **GPEDIT.MSC** and press enter key.
4. On **Local Group Policy Editor** snap-in under **Computer Configuration** expand **Administrative Templates** and expand **Network**.
5. From the expanded list click **Offline Files** and from the right pane double click **Synchronize offline files before suspend**.

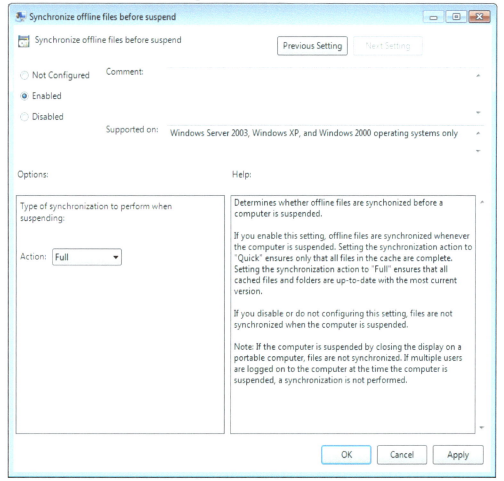

6. On the opened box select **Enabled** radio button and in the **Options** section from the drop-down list make sure that **Full** option is selected.

7. Once done, click **Ok** button to accept and confirm your configuration and close **Local Group Policy Editor** snap-in.

8. Open **Command Prompt** and the command window type **GPUPDATE /FORCE** to update your computer with latest settings.

9. Close **Command Prompt**.

Delete Temporary Offline Files When Users Logoff

When users work with offline files temporary files are created which are stored on local hard disk of the computers. If, because of any reason computer shuts down instantaneously, these temporary files get permanently stored on the hard disk and occupy disk space. With the help of group policy settings in Windows 7 administrators can eliminate this problem by configuring deletion of temporary offline files from the local computers when users logoff. As an administrator you can configure this by following the steps given below:

1. Log on to the computer with administrator account.

2. Click **Start** button.

3. At the bottom of start menu in search box type **GPEDIT.MSC** and press enter key.

4. On **Local Group Policy Editor** snap-in under **Computer Configuration** expand **Administrative Templates** and expand **Network**.

5. From the expanded list click **Offline Files** and from the right pane double click **At logoff, delete local copy of user's offline files**.

6. On the opened box select **Enabled** radio button and in the **Options** section check **Delete only the temporary offline files** checkbox.

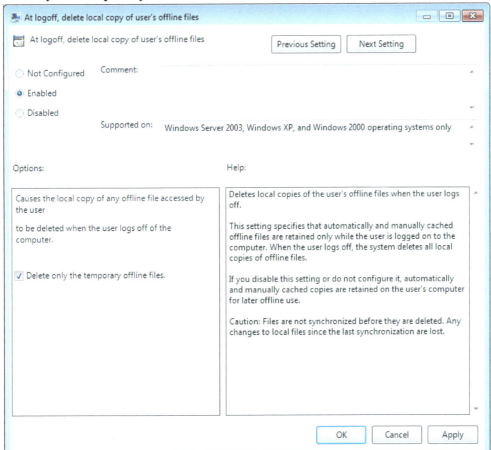

7. Once done, click **Ok** button to accept and confirm your configuration and close **Local Group Policy Editor** snap-in.

8. Open **Command Prompt.**

9. In the command window type **GPUPDATE /FORCE** to update your computer with latest settings.

10. Close **Command Prompt**.

Prevent Taking Specific File Types Offline

In home environments users can take almost any file type offline so that it can become accessible to them in case remote location is not available. On the contrary in production environments sometimes administrators might not want users to work on specific file types offline. When this is the case they can prevent the file types from getting cached on the local computers. This filtering can be done on the basis of file extensions. As an administrator you can configure this group policy setting by following the steps given below:

1. Log on to the computer with administrator account.

2. Click **Start** button.

3. At the bottom of start menu in search box type **GPEDIT.MSC** and press enter key.

4. On **Local Group Policy Editor** snap-in under **Computer Configuration** expand **Administrative Templates** and expand **Network**.

5. From the expanded list click **Offline Files** and from the right pane double click **Files not cached**.

6. On the opened box select **Enabled** radio button and in the **Options** section in the available text box type the extensions of the file types which you want to prevent from getting cached. Extensions should be prefixed by the asterisk (*) sign and should be separated with commas. (For example *.pdf, *.bmp)

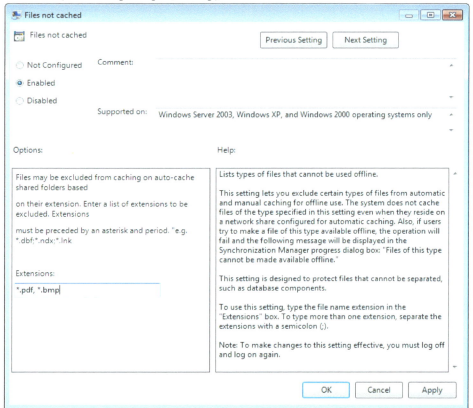

7. Once done, click **Ok** button to accept and confirm your configuration and close **Local Group Policy Editor** snap-in.

8. Open **Command Prompt.**

9. In the command window type **GPUPDATE /FORCE** to update your computer with latest settings.

10. Close **Command Prompt**.

Define Default Offline Files Cache Size

When a user works with offline files Windows 7 by default caches the files on the system drive of local hard disk. Default size that is consumed by the caching of offline files is 10% of the total drive. In some cases, however administrators may want to reduce or increase this limitation as per the requirements of the organizations or homes. As an administrator if you want to modify this setting you need to follow the steps given below:

1. Log on to the computer with administrator account.

2. Click **Start** button.

3. At the bottom of start menu in search box type **GPEDIT.MSC** and press enter key.

4. On **Local Group Policy Editor** snap-in under **Computer Configuration** expand **Administrative Templates** and expand **Network**.

5. From the expanded list click **Offline Files** and from the right pane double click **Default cache size.**

6. On the opened box select **Enabled** radio button and in the **Options** section in available text box specify the amount of disk space you want to assign for caching of offline files. Pattern to be used is: 1500 = 15% (15.00%), 2050 = 20.5% (20.50%).

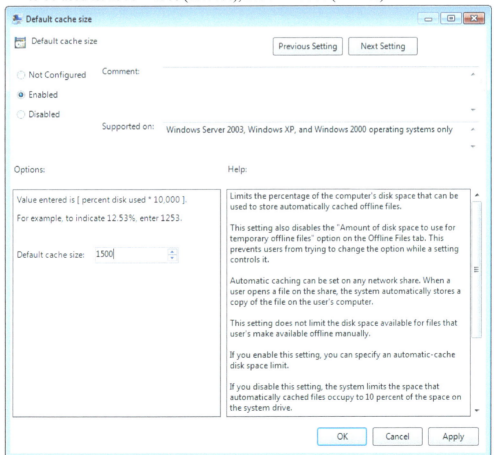

7. Once done, click **Ok** button to accept and confirm your configuration and close **Local Group Policy Editor** snap-in.

8. Open **Command Prompt** and the command window type **GPUPDATE /FORCE** to update your computer with latest settings.

9. Close **Command Prompt**.

Disable Offline Files Feature

When users are connected to the network in any production environment at home, files they mostly used can be scattered among all computers available on the network. In order to make scattered files Microsoft Windows provide easily accessible Offline Files feature. However for security reasons administrators may sometimes want to disable this feature. Disabling Offline Files ensures that the files are secured and the chances of files getting cached and stolen are reduced. As an administrator if you want to disable Offline Files feature you need to follow the steps given below:

1. Log on to the computer with administrator account.

2. Click **Start** button.

3. At the bottom of start menu in search box type **GPEDIT.MSC** and press enter key.

4. On **Local Group Policy Editor** snap-in under **Computer Configuration** expand **Administrative Templates** and expand **Network**.

5. From the expanded list click **Offline Files** and from the right pane double click **Allow or Disallow use of the Offline Files feature.**

6. On the opened box select **Disabled** radio button and click **Ok** button to accept and confirm your configuration.

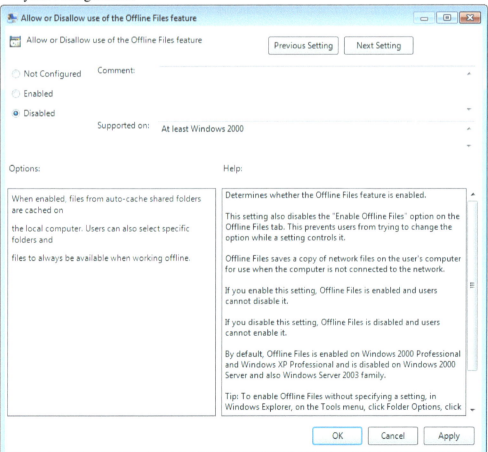

7. Close **Local Group Policy Editor** snap-in.

8. Open **Command Prompt** and the command window type **GPUPDATE /FORCE** to update your computer with latest settings.

9. Close **Command Prompt**.

Restrict Users from Changing Desktop Wallpaper

Almost every organization has its own logo and it wants that the logo should be displayed as default desktop wallpaper on every computer in its office. Also, these companies want that users should not have permissions to change desktop wallpaper at their own will. This can easily be done by following the instructions given below:

1. Click **Start** button.
2. At the bottom of the menu in the search box type **GPEDIT.MSC**.
3. In the **Local Computer Policy** snap-in under **Computer Configuration** expand **Administrative Templates** tree.
4. Expand **Control Panel** tree.
5. Select **User Accounts**
6. In the right pane double-click **Apply default user logon picture for all users**.
7. In the opened window select **Enabled** radio button to restrict users from changing desktop wallpaper.

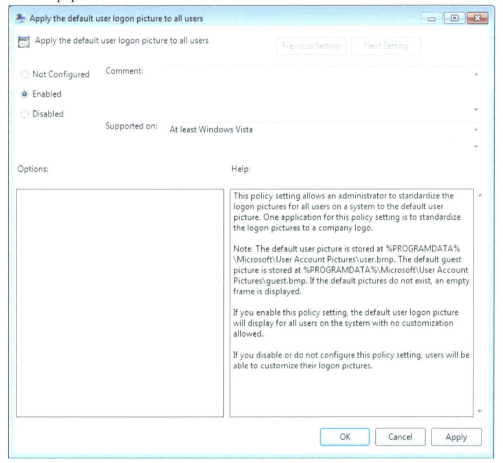

8. Click **Ok** button to accept and confirm your selection.

9. Close **Local Computer Policy** snap-in.

10. Click **Start** button and go to **All Programs**.

11. From the list select **Accessories**.

12. Right-click **Command Prompt** and select **Run as Administrator**.

13. In the **User Account Control** dialog box click **Ok** button to allow Windows to use your administrative credentials to run the program.

14. In the **Administrator: Command Prompt** window type **GPUPDATE /FORCE** and press enter key.

Disable Control Panel

Whether you are a home computer user or you are in an office where IT security means a lot, Control Panel is the place from where anyone can modify computer settings and make it vulnerable to risks. Therefore when a single PC is shared among many users it is strongly recommended that Control Panel should be disabled to provide an extra layer of security to the machine and data it contains. Process to disable access to Control Panel is quite simple and is given below:

1. Click **Start** button.

2. At the bottom of the menu in the search box type **GPEDIT.MSC**.

3. In the **Local Computer Policy** snap-in under **User Configuration** expand **Administrative Templates** tree and select **Control Panel**.

4. In the right pane double-click **Prohibit Access to the Control Panel**.

5. From the opened window select **Enabled** radio button.

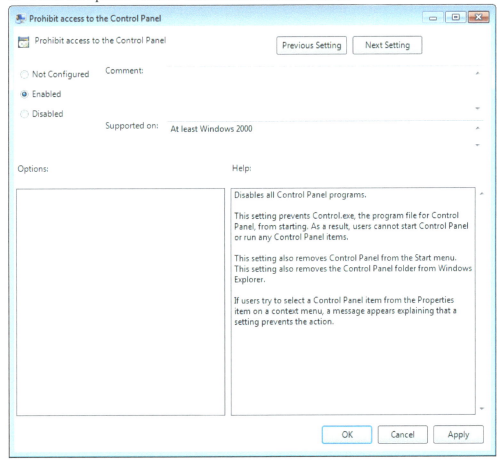

6. Click **Ok** button to accept and confirm your selection.

7. Close **Local Computer Policy** snap-in.

8. Click **Start** button and go to **All Programs**.

9. From the list select **Accessories**.

10. Right-click **Command Prompt** and select **Run as Administrator**.

11. In the **User Account Control** dialog box click **Ok** button to allow Windows to use your administrative credentials to run the program.

12. In the **Administrator: Command Prompt** window type **GPUPDATE /FORCE** and press enter key.

Allow Users or Groups to Change Clock Time

When Windows 7 or any other post Windows 98 Microsoft operating system is installed, by default only administrators are allowed to change system time. If a person does not belong to Administrators group he cannot change the system time until he is authorized to do so by the administrators. Administrators can authorize any user or group to change system time by modifying group policies of the local system. In order to do so administrators need to follow the steps given below:

1. Log on to the computer with administrator's account.

2. Click **Start** button.

3. At the bottom of start menu in search box type **GPEDIT.MSC** command and press enter key.

4. On **Local Computer Policy** snap in under **Computer Configuration** expand **Windows Settings**.

5. From the list expand **Security Settings**.

6. Expand **Local Policies** and click **User Rights Assignment**.

7. From the right pane double click **Change the system time**.

8. On **Change the system time Properties** box click **Add users or groups** button.

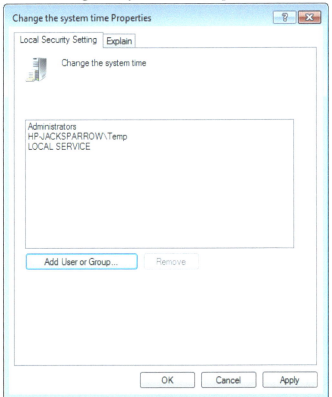

9. On **Select Users or Groups** box under **Enter the object names to select** list box type the name of the user or group to which you want to assign the permission and click **Ok** button.

10. Back on **Change the system time Properties** box click **Ok** button to confirm your configuration and close **Local Group Policy** snap-in.

11. Open **Command Prompt** and in the command window type **GPUPDATE /FORCE** command to update the computer with new group policy settings.

12. Close command window.

No 'Change Password' Option on Ctrl+Alt+Del

By-default Windows 7 allows all users to change their passwords on their own. This configuration might be ideal in home environment or for any small-scale industry. However, if a Windows 7 computer is used in medium or large scale industry administrators would not want users to change their passwords themselves by pressing Ctrl+Alt+Del keys. On the contrary they would like to manage this feature using group policies. If in any industry Windows 7 computer is running in a workgroup environment administrators can remove Change Password option when Ctrl+Alt+Del keys are pressed by following the steps given below:

1. Log on to the computer with administrator account.
2. Click **Start** button.
3. At the bottom of start menu in search box type **GPEDIT.MSC** command and press enter key.
4. On the opened **Local Group Policy Editor** snap-in under **User Configuration** expand **Administrative Templates** and then expand **System**.
5. Click **Ctrl+Alt+Del** Options and from the right pane double click **Remove Change Password**.

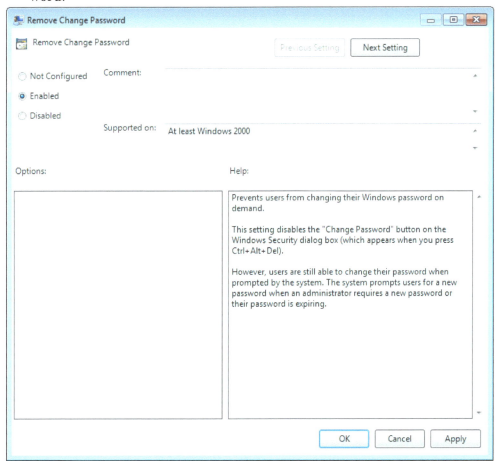

6. On the opened box select **Enabled** radio button and click **Ok** button to accept your configuration.

7. Close **Local Group Policy Editor** snap-in and open **Command Prompt**.

8. On the command window type **GPUPDATE /FORCE** command to update your current computer configuration with latest settings.

9. Close **Command Prompt.**

More Info:

With the help of above configuration, administrators can only remove Change Password option when Ctrl+Alt+Del keys are pressed. Users will still be able to change their passwords by going to Control Panel.

Accept Blank Passwords While Network Access

To make computers secure by default Windows 7 does not allow users to log on from the network if they have not set their account passwords. This means that whenever a user wants to access the computer remotely, that is from the network, he needs to specify the password for his user account without which Windows 7 would straight away deny the access. However, in home environments where there are not more than two or three computers users can remove this restriction considering that in homes computers are not at risks. You can remove blank password restriction by following the steps given below:

1. Log on to the computer with administrator account.

2. Click **Start** button.

3. At bottom of start menu in search box type **GPEDIT.MSC** command and press enter key.

4. On **Local Group Policy Editor** snap-in under **Computer Configuration** expand **Windows Settings** and then expand **Security Settings**.

5. Expand **Local Policies** and click **Security Options**.

6. From the right pane double click on **Accounts: Limit local account use blank passwords to console logon only** and from the opened box select **Disabled** radio button.

7. Once done, click **Ok** button and close **Local Group Policy Editor** snap-in.

8. Open **Command Prompt** and in command window type **GPUPDATE /FORCE** to update here computer policy with latest configuration.

9. Close **Command Prompt**.

Manage Reversible Password Encryption

In Windows platform, by default user accounts and their passwords are stored in Security Accounts Manager (SAM) file and are stored in encrypted form. Encryption algorithm of Microsoft Windows is quite strong and is not easily breakable. However in scenarios where network consists of multivendor operating systems, for example Sun Solaris, Linux, Novell NetWare, etc. administrators may want to allow users to log on from any computer with non-Windows operating system installed on it. This is only possible when the algorithm which is used to encrypt user accounts and passwords is either understood by other vendors' operating systems or is weak enough so that it can easily be reversed. On Microsoft Windows platform administrators can configure group policy settings to store user account passwords with reversible encryption so that other vendors' operating systems can easily decrypt them and can authenticate users to log on using those computers. If you are an administrator you can configure the above settings by following the steps below:

1. Log on to the computer with administrator account.
2. Click **Start** button.
3. At the bottom of start menu in search box type **GPEDIT.MSC** command and press enter key.
4. On **Local Group Policy Editor** snap-in under **Computer Configuration** expand **Windows Settings** and then expand **Security Settings**.
5. From the opened list expand **Account Policies** and from the list click **Password Policies**.

6. From the right pane, double click **Store password using reversible encryption** and from the opened box in select **Enabled** radio button.

7. Click **Ok** button to accept and confirm your configuration and close **Local Group Policy Editor** snap-in.

8. Open **Command Prompt** and in command window type **GPUPDATE /FORCE** to update here computer policy with latest configuration.

9. Close **Command Prompt**.

Encrypting Offline Files Cache

In home environments where users are trusted, default configuration of Windows 7 is quite ideal and need not to be modified. However when working in medium or large scale industries, that is, in production environments security is one of the major concerns which all administrators must keep in minds. Because of security reasons every communication that takes place between two machines, even in local area network, is encrypted. Same is the case with offline files cache. When sensitive files are made available for offline use it becomes essential for client computers to maintain the security of those files. Administrators can encrypt offline files cache on a Windows 7 computer to protect the cached files from any mishaps. The process of encrypting offline files cache on Windows 7 computers is given below:

1. Log on to the computer with administrator account.
2. Click **Start** button.
3. At the bottom of start menu in search box type **GPEDIT.MSC** and press enter key.
4. On **Local Group Policy Editor** snap-in under **Computer Configuration** expand **Administrative Templates** and expand **Network**.
5. From the expanded list click **Offline Files** and from the right pane double click **Encrypt the Offline Files cache.**

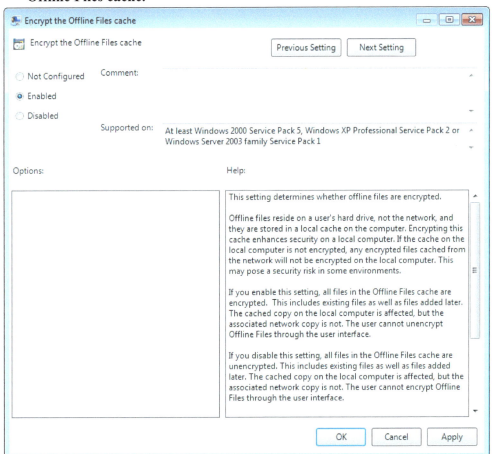

6. On the opened box select **Enabled** radio button and click **Ok** button to accept and confirm your configuration.

7. Close **Local Group Policy Editor** snap-in.

8. Open **Command Prompt** and the command window type **GPUPDATE /FORCE** to update your computer with latest settings.

9. Close **Command Prompt**.

Prevent Users from Installing Shared Printers

In medium or large scale industries where there are several printers shared on the network, Windows 7 users are by default allowed to download and install drivers for the shared printers without any administrative privileges. This feature makes administrators' tasks quite easy as they do not have to grant every user or group the permissions to install shared printer drivers on their computers. However in some cases administrators may not want this configuration because of security reasons and to prevent printers from getting misused by the users. As an administrator you can configure this by following the steps given below:

1. Log on to the computer with administrator account.
2. Click **Start** button.
3. At bottom of start menu in search box type **GPEDIT.MSC** command and press enter key.
4. On **Local Group Policy Editor** snap-in under **Computer Configuration** expand **Windows Settings** and then expand **Security Settings**.
5. Expand **Local Policies** and click **Security Options**.
6. From the right pane double click **Devices: Prevent users from installing printer drivers** and on the opened box select **Enabled** radio button.

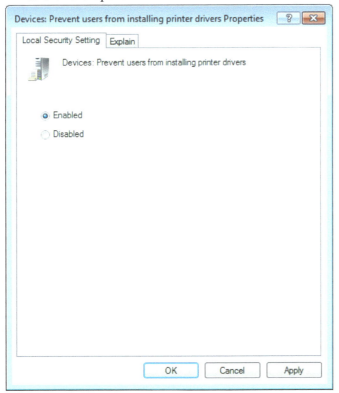

7. Once done, click **Ok** button and close **Local Group Policy Editor** snap-in.

8. Open **Command Prompt** and in command window type **GPUPDATE /FORCE** to update here computer policy with latest configuration.

9. Close **Command Prompt**.

Allow Users/Groups to Take Objects' Ownership

By-default only administrators are allowed to take ownership of any file or folder present on a Windows 7 computer. However administrators may sometimes need to delegate the task of taking ownership to any other user or group in order to reduce some overhead. This configuration requires modification in group policy and the steps to do so are given below:

1. Log on to the computer with administrator's account.

2. Click **Start** button.

3. At the bottom of start menu in search box type **GPEDIT.MSC** command and press enter key.

4. On **Local Computer Policy** snap in under **Computer Configuration** expand **Windows Settings**.

5. From the list expand **Security Settings**.

6. Expand **Local Policies** and click **User Rights Assignment**.

7. From the right pane double click **Take ownership of files and other objects**.

8. On **Take ownership of files and other objects Properties** box click **Add user or group** button.

9. On **Select Users or Groups** box under **Enter the object names to select** list box type the name of the user or group to which you want to delegate the task and click **Ok** button.

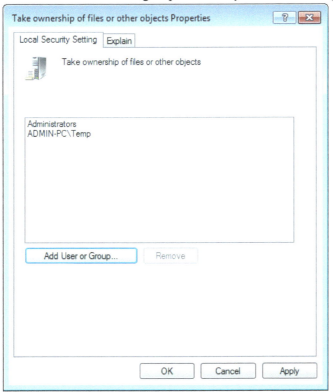

10. Back **Take ownership of files and other objects Properties** box click **Ok** button to confirm your configuration and close **Local Group Policy** snap-in.

11. Open **Command Prompt** and in the command window type **GPUPDATE /FORCE** command to update the computer with new group policy settings.

12. Close command window.

Disable Autoplay for All Users

Whenever you insert a CD/DVD or any other storage media in your computer Windows 7 automatically detects it and displays its contents by opening a new window in Windows Explorer. This is a great feature that Windows 7 offers. However, there might be times when this feature makes your computer vulnerable to virus attacks. This is because when you insert a CD or DVD Windows 7 starts detecting its contents and finally it opens the contents of the media in a new window. Suppose the CD/DVD or flash drive that you have inserted had virus in it. In this case virus residing in the media will be self-executed and will infect your system within fraction of seconds. Therefore sometimes it is recommended to disable Autoplay feature to prevent your computer from getting infected with virus accidentally. Process to turn off Autoplay feature is given below:

1. Click **Start** button.
2. At the bottom of the menu in the search box type **GPEDIT.MSC**.
3. In the **Local Computer Policy** snap-in under **Computer Configuration** expand **Administrative Templates** tree.
4. Expand **Windows Components** tree and select **AutoPlay Policies.**
5. In the right pane double click **Turn off Autoplay**.

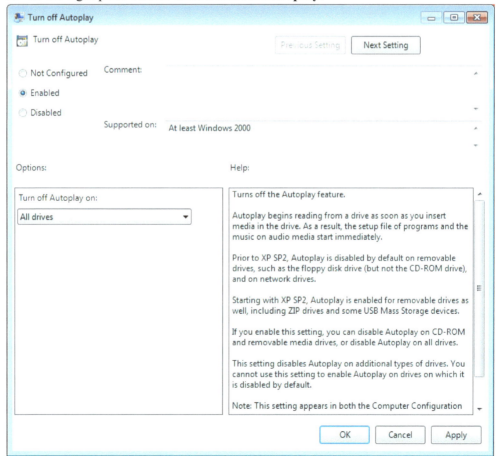

6. In the opened window select **Enabled** radio button to disable Autoplay feature.

7. Click **Ok** button to accept and confirm your selection.

8. Close **Local Computer Policy** snap-in.

9. Click **Start** button and go to **All Programs**.

10. From the list select **Accessories**.

11. Right-click on **Command Prompt** and select **Run as Administrator**.

12. In the **User Account Control** dialog box click **Ok** button to allow Windows to use your administrative credentials to run the program.

13. In the **Administrator: Command Prompt** window type **GPUPDATE /FORCE** and press enter key.

You can test your configuration by inserting any CD/DVD or USB Pen Drive in your computer.

Hide and Restrict Access to C: Drive

If you are connected to the Internet regularly either at your homes or in offices you are always vulnerable to virus attacks or unauthorized accesses. You can negate this loophole by hiding and restricting access to C: drive which will prevent your computer from any unauthorized access and will also protect it from malicious and/or harmful virus attacks.

You can hide and restrict access to C: drive by following the below given steps:

1. Click **Start** button.
2. At the bottom of the start menu in the search box type **GPEDIT.MSC**.
3. In the **Local Computer Policy** snap-in under **User Configuration** expand **Administrative Templates**.
4. Expand **Windows Components** and select **Windows Explorer**.
5. In the right pane double-click **Hide these specified drives in My Computer**.
6. In the opened box select **Enabled** radio button and under **Options** frame from the drop-down list choose **Restrict C drive only**.
7. Click **Ok** button to accept and confirm your selection.

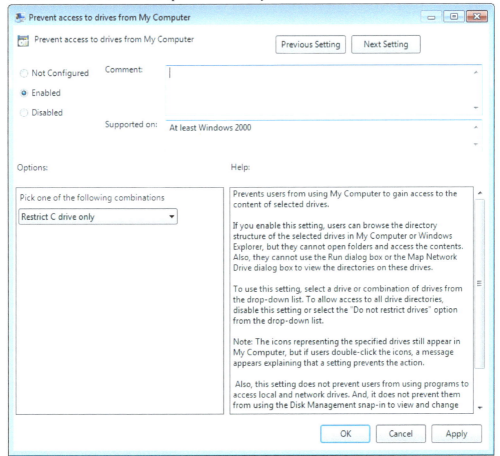

8. Then double-click **Prevent access to drives from My Computer**..

9. From the opened box select **Enabled** radio button and under **Options** frame from the drop-down list select **Restrict C drive only**

10. Click **Ok** button to accept and confirm your selection.

11. Close **Local Computer Policy** snap-in.

12. Click **Start** button and go to **All Programs**.

13. From the list select **Accessories**.

14. Right-click **Command Prompt** and select **Run as Administrator**.

15. In the **User Account Control** dialog box click **Ok** button to allow Windows to use your administrative credentials to run the program.

16. In the **Administrator: Command Prompt** window type **GPUPDATE /FORCE** and press enter key.

You can verify this configuration by going to **My Computer**. You will find that there is no C: available. Even if you want to open this drive by typing C: in the address bar of Windows Explorer you will be displayed with a message saying access denied.

Allow Access to CDs/DVDs to Locally Users Only

By default network users can access almost any drive on the system using Universal Naming Convention (UNC) path and if the drive is protected by administrative share it can be accessed by typing the UNC path followed by $ and providing administrative credentials when prompted. This configuration is applicable on CD/DVD ROM as well. However in some cases, say in typical network environments, administrators may want to restrict this feature for various security reasons. As an administrator if you want to configure this setting on your Windows 7 computer you need to follow the steps given below:

1. Log on to the computer with administrator account.
2. Click **Start** button.
3. At bottom of start menu in search box type **GPEDIT.MSC** command and press enter key.
4. On **Local Group Policy Editor** snap-in under **Computer Configuration** expand **Windows Settings** and then expand **Security Settings**.
5. Expand **Local Policies** and click **Security Options**.
6. From the right pane double click **Devices: Restrict CD-ROM access to locally logged-on user only** and on the opened box select **Enabled** radio button.

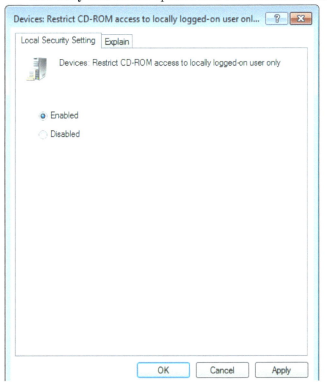

7. Once done, click **Ok** button and close **Local Group Policy Editor** snap-in.
8. Open **Command Prompt** and in command window type **GPUPDATE /FORCE** to update here computer policy with latest configuration.
9. Close **Command Prompt**.

Allow Users Format/Eject Removable NTFS Media

As default nature of Windows 7 only administrators are allowed to format and/or eject any removable media that has NTFS file system. This default nature is quite ideal in production environments where administrators need to restrict users from misusing the media. However in homes this security configuration is not required at all and therefore administrators, which are home users, can remove this restriction and allow all users to format removable media at their own will. As an administrator you can configure this setting by following the steps given below:

1. Log on to the computer with administrator account.

2. Click **Start** button.

3. At bottom of start menu in search box type **GPEDIT.MSC** command and press enter key.

4. On **Local Group Policy Editor** snap-in under **Computer Configuration** expand **Windows Settings** and then expand **Security Settings**.

5. Expand **Local Policies** and click **Security Options**.

6. From the right pane double click on **Devices: Allowed to format and eject removable media** and on the opened box from the drop-down list select **Administrators and Interactive Users**.

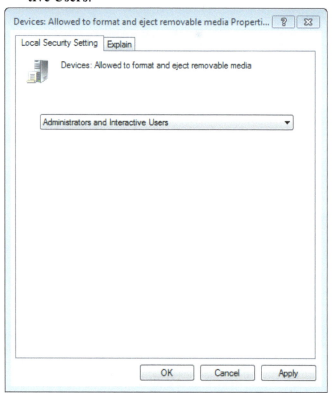

7. Once done, click **Ok** button and close **Local Group Policy Editor** snap-in.

8. Open **Command Prompt** and in command window type **GPUPDATE /FORCE** to update here computer policy with latest configuration.

9. Close **Command Prompt**.

Disable All External Mass Storage Devices

There are cases when you don't want users to insert any external media in the systems. Whether it is a USB flash drive or a CD/DVD ROM, every external storage device makes your machine vulnerable to risks. Also, many companies keep external storage device detection disabled in their office PCs for security purposes. In other words, disabling external storage detection on shared computers is strongly recommended by security professionals.

Process to disable all external storage media devices computer is as below:

1. Click **Start** button.

2. At the bottom of the menu in the search box type **GPEDIT.MSC**.

3. In the **Local Group Policy Editor** snap-in under **Computer Configuration** expand **Administrative Templates** tree.

4. Expand **System** sub-tree.

5. Select **Removable Storage Access** from **System** sub-tree.

6. In the right pane double click **All Removable Storage classes: Deny all access**.

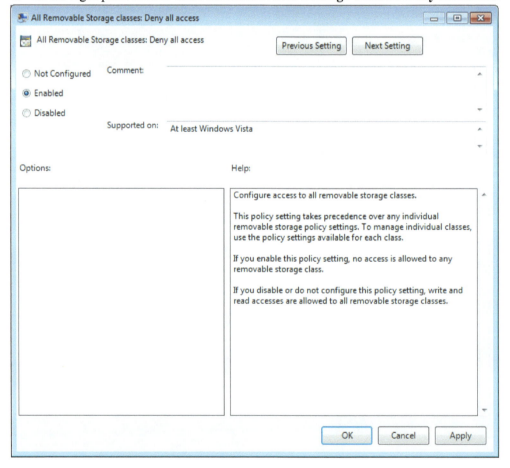

7. In **All Removable Storage classes: Deny all access** window select **Enabled** radio button to enable restriction.

8. Click **Ok** button to accept and confirm your selection.

9. Close **Local Group Policy Editor** snap-in.

10. Click **Start** button and go to **All Programs**.

11. From the list select **Accessories**.

12. Right-click on **Command Prompt** and select **Run as Administrator**.

13. On **User Account Control** dialog box click **Yes** button to allow Windows to use administrative credentials to run the program.

14. In the **Administrator: Command Prompt** window type **GPUPDATE /FORCE** and press enter key.

Check your latest configuration by inserting a USB flash drive in a USB port. When you will try to access the device you will be displayed with message box telling that your access is denied.

Prevent Data Backing up on Optical Media

In every scenario backing up data is a major aspect that is taken quite seriously. It is considered that without backup no organization can function smoothly. Administrators are specialized in planning backup strategies and are also well versed with the process of restoring backups in case any disaster occurs. Normally data is backed up either on a network location or on any backup storage media. In some cases backup is also stored on optical media, hence exposing the backup file to potential risks. In order to eliminate these risks administrators can restrict backing up data on any optical media. As an administrator you can do so by following the steps given below:

1. Log on to the computer with administrator account.

2. Click **Start** button.

3. At the bottom of start menu in search box type **GPEDIT.MSC** and press enter key.

4. On **Local Group Policy Editor** snap-in under **Computer Configuration** expand **Administrative Templates** and expand **Windows Components**.

5. Expand **Backup** and click **Client**.

6. In the right pane double click **Prevent backing up to optical media (CD/DVD)** and in the opened window select **Enabled** radio button.

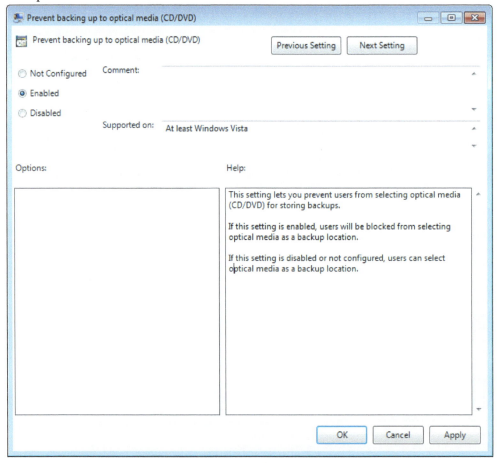

7. Click **Ok** button to accept and confirm your configuration and close **Local Group Policy Editor** snap-in.

8. Open **Command Prompt** and the command window type **GPUPDATE /FORCE** to update your computer with latest settings.

9. Close **Command Prompt**.

Enable BitLocker without TPM Chip

By-default Windows 7 allows administrators to enable BitLocker only when Trusted Platform Module (TPM) chip is present and is enabled in the bios settings of the computer. However, this feature of Windows 7 can be modified through Group Policies and BitLocker can still be enabled without TPM support. In order to do so administrators need to follow the below instructions:

1. Click **Start** button.

2. At the bottom of start menu in search box type **GPEDIT.MSC**.

3. In the **Local Computer Policy** snap-in under **Computer Configuration** expand **Administrative Templates**.

4. Expand **Windows Companies**.

5. Expand **BitLocker Drive Encryption**.

6. Select **Operating System Drives**.

7. In the right pane double click **Require additional authentication at startup**.

8. In the opened window select **Enabled** radio button.

9. Under **Options** frame in the left side of the window check **Allow BitLocker without a Compatible TPM** checkbox.

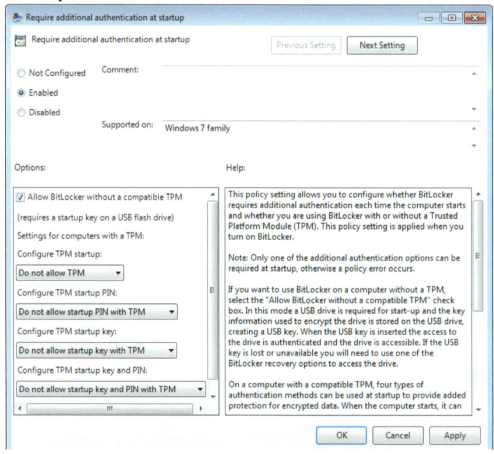

10. From the below four drop down lists select **Do not allow TPM** in **Configure TPM Startup**, **Do not allow startup PIN with TPM** in **Configure TPM startup PIN**, **Do not allow startup key with TPM** in **Configure TPM startup key** and **Allow startup key and PIN with TPM** in **Configure TPM startup key and PIN**.

11. Click **Ok** button to accept and confirm your selection.

12. Close **Local Computer Policy** snap-in.

13. Click **Start** button and go to **All Programs**.

14. From the list select **Accessories**.

15. Right-click on **Command Prompt** and select **Run as Administrator**.

16. In the **User Account Control** dialog box click **Ok** button to allow Windows to use your administrative credentials to run the program.

17. In the **Administrator: Command Prompt** window type **GPUPDATE /FORCE** and press enter key.

Manage BitLocker for Removable Storage Media

BitLocker is the feature which needs to be enabled on individual drives in case administrators want to protect data available on desktop PCs or on laptops. Though administrators can do so quite easily, however when it comes to removable storage media things should be taken seriously. This is because removable storage media can be used to steal sensitive information from the office computers. Therefore, for security purposes administrators may want to revoke users' privileges of turning on BitLocker on removable storage media. As an administrator you can do so by following the steps given below:

1. Log on to the computer with administrator account.

2. Click **Start** button.

3. At the bottom of start menu in search box type **GPEDIT.MSC** and press enter key.

4. On **Local Group Policy Editor** snap-in under **Computer Configuration** expand **Administrative Templates** and expand **Windows Components**.

5. Expand **BitLocker Drive Encryption** and from expanded list select **Removable Data Drives**.

6. From the right pane double click **Control use of BitLocker on removable drives**.

7. On the opened window select **Disabled** radio button and click **Ok** button to accept and confirm your configuration.

8. Close **Local Group Policy Editor** snap-in and open **Command Prompt**.

9. In command window type **GPUPDATE /FORCE** and press enter key to update your computer configuration with latest settings.

10. Close **Command Prompt**.

No Saving on Non-BitLocker Removable Media

By default Windows 7 allows all users to write data on any removable storage media which is attached to the computer. In home environments this configuration is fair enough and should not be modified. However in production environments where there are several computers in the network and every computer contains highly sensitive data, security becomes one of the major concerns. Administrators in these cases may want to control BitLocker permissions even on removable storage media devices to protect the organizations from any mishaps. As an administrator you can enforce any removable storage media to be mounted as a read only if it is not protected by BitLocker drive encryption by following the steps given below:

1. Log on to the computer with administrator account.
2. Click **Start** button.
3. At the bottom of start menu in search box type **GPEDIT.MSC** and press enter key.
4. On **Local Group Policy Editor** snap-in under **Computer Configuration** expand **Administrative Templates** and expand **Windows Components**.
5. Expand **BitLocker Drive Encryption** and from expanded list select **Removable Data Drives**.

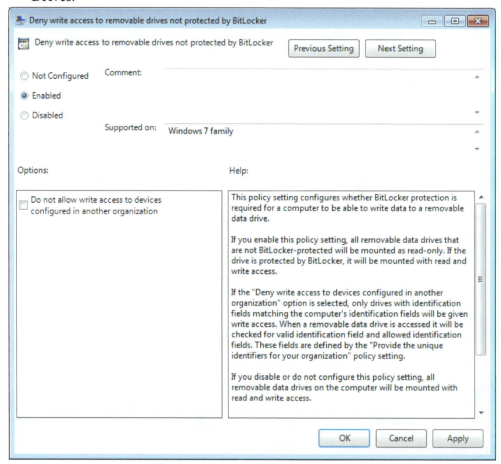

6. From the right pane double click **Deny write access to removable drives not protected by BitLocker**.

7. On the opened window select **Enabled** radio button and click **Ok** button to accept and confirm your configuration.

8. Close **Local Group Policy Editor** snap-in and open **Command Prompt**.

9. In command window type **GPUPDATE /FORCE** and press enter key to update your computer configuration with latest settings.

10. Close **Command Prompt**.

Manage Use of Biometrics

When Windows 7 is installed, by default it accepts all biometric authentication methods to make user logon process easier. In order to use biometrics feature a biometrics sensor device (hardware peripheral) is required. In case biometrics sensor is not available on any computer, especially in production environment, it is strongly recommended that administrators should disable the use of biometrics devices to environment secure the network infrastructure. If Windows 7 computer is in a workgroup environment administrators need to disable this feature by configuring group policy settings on each computer. The process of disabling the use of biometrics device is given below:

1. Log on to the computer with administrator account.
2. Click **Start** button.
3. At the bottom of start menu in search box type **GPEDIT.MSC** and press enter key.
4. On **Local Group Policy Editor** snap-in under **Computer Configuration** expand **Administrative Templates** and expand **Windows Components**.
5. From the expanded list click **Biometrics** and from the right pane double click **Allow the use of biometrics**.

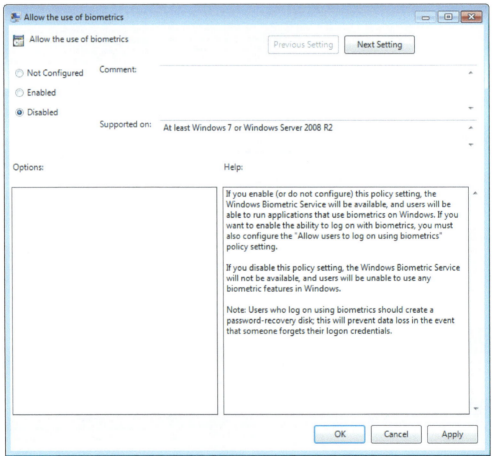

6. On the opened window select **Disabled** radio button and click **Ok** button to accept and confirm your configuration.

7. Close **Local Group Policy Editor** snap-in and open **Command Prompt**.

8. In command window type **GPUPDATE /FORCE** and press enter key to update your computer configuration with latest settings.

9. Close **Command Prompt**.

Apply Group Policy Filtering

When administrators apply group policies on any computer, they become applicable for all users on that particular system. However there might be cases when administrators may not want group policies to affect some users or groups and become applicable for others at the same time. When this is the case administrators can use group policy filtering to allow group policies to take effect on the users and groups which they specify. As an administrator you can apply group policy filtering by following the steps given below:

1. Log on to the computer with administrator account and make sure that you have configured your computer to display all hidden files and folders.

2. Click **Start** button.

3. At the bottom of start menu in search box type **%systemroot%\System32\GroupPolicy** and press enter key.

4. On the opened window right click **gpt.ini** file and from the menu click **Properties**.

5. On the opened box go to **Security** tab and click **Edit** button.

6. On the appeared box click **Add** button to add user or group for which you want to apply group policy filter.

7. Once done, select the newly added user or group from the list and under **Permissions** list check **Full Control** checkbox below **Deny** column.

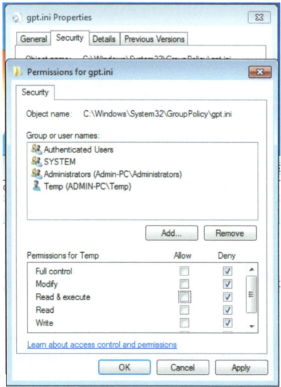

8. Click **Ok** button on all opened windows and open **Command Prompt**.

9. In the command window type **GPUPDATE /FORCE** and press enter key to update new group policy configuration.

10. Close **Command Prompt**.

Permit Users or Groups to Restore from Backups

In Windows operating system by default Backup Operators and Administrators are allowed to backup and restore files, folders and/or system state of the computer. For home PCs or small scale industries this configuration is ideal and does not require any modifications. However, when the company is large and has thousands of users and several administrators, responsibility of restoring from backups can be delegated to other users or groups which the organization has hired for the purpose. If you are an administrator you can permit users or groups to restore data from backups by following the steps given below:

1. Log on to the computer with administrator's account.

2. Click **Start** button.

3. At the bottom of start menu in search box type **GPEDIT.MSC** command and press enter key.

4. On **Local Computer Policy** snap in under **Computer Configuration** expand **Windows Settings**.

5. From the list expand **Security Settings**.

6. Expand **Local Policies** and click **User Rights Assignment**.

7. From the right pane double click **Restore files and directories**.

8. On **Restore files and directories Properties** box select **Backup Operators** group and click on **Remove** button to revoke its restore permissions.

9. Click **Add User or Group** button.

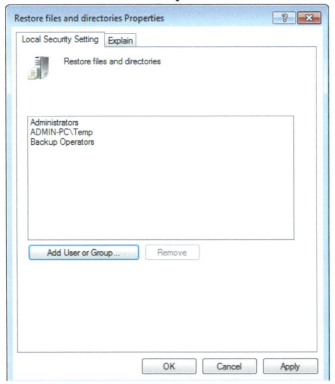

10. On **Select Users or Groups** box under **Enter the object names to select** box type the name of the user or group you want to grant restore permission and click **Ok** button.

11. Back on **Restore files and directories Properties** box click **Ok** button to confirm your configuration and close **Local Group Policy** snap-in.

12. Open **Command Prompt** and in the command window type **GPUPDATE /FORCE** command to update the computer with new group policy settings.

13. Close command window.

Preventing System Restore Point Creation

Whenever a new device is installed on a Windows 7 computer and it starts installing its drivers, Windows 7 automatically creates a restore point to ensure that the computer becomes fault-tolerant in case the device driver fails to initialize. System restore point is also created automatically when any other uncommon device activity takes place. System restore point creation process, of course, consumes some processing speed and eats a bit of memory as well. However in home environments where there are one or two computers and security is not a major issue, people may want to disable this restore point creation process in order to enhance Windows 7 performance. If you want to configure this you need to follow the steps given below:

1. Log on to the computer with administrator account.

2. Click **Start** button.

3. At the bottom of start menu in search box type **GPEDIT.MSC** and press enter key.

4. On **Local Group Policy Editor** snap-in under **Computer Configuration** expand **Administrative Templates** and expand **System**.

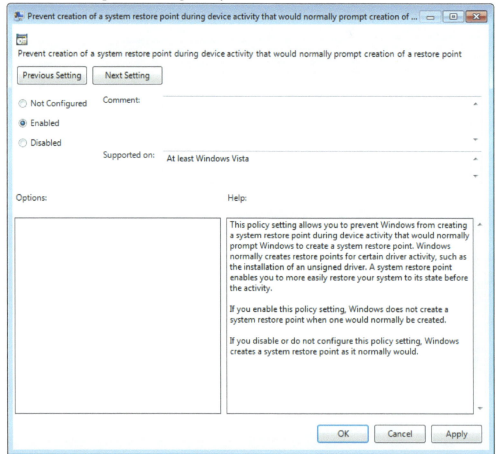

5. From expanded list select **Device Installation** from the right pane double click **Prevent creation of a system restore point during device activity that would normally prompt creation of a restore point** and on the opened window select **Enabled** radio button.

6. Once done click **Ok** button to accept and confirm your configuration.

7. Close **Local Group Policy Editor** snap-in and open **Command Prompt**.

8. In command window type **GPUPDATE /FORCE** and press enter key to update your computer configuration with latest settings.

9. Close **Command Prompt**.

Disable Backup Feature

Backup plays an important role in every network setup. Without backups organizations are always considered at risks. There are numerous strategies that administrators plan for backup and restoration pro4cesses and administrators are provided special training for the purpose. However in some cases administrators might not want the backup feature to be left enabled at all. Reason behind this can be internal security threats or to provide extreme security to the sensitive data. When this is the case administrators can follow the steps given below in order to disable backup feature on a Windows 7 computer:

1. Log on to the computer with administrator account.

2. Click **Start** button.

3. At the bottom of start menu in search box type **GPEDIT.MSC** and press enter key.

4. On **Local Group Policy Editor** snap-in under **Computer Configuration** expand **Administrative Templates** and expand **Windows Components**.

5. Expand **Backup** and click **Client**.

6. In the right pane, double click **Turn off the ability to back up data files** and in the opened window select **Enabled** radio button.

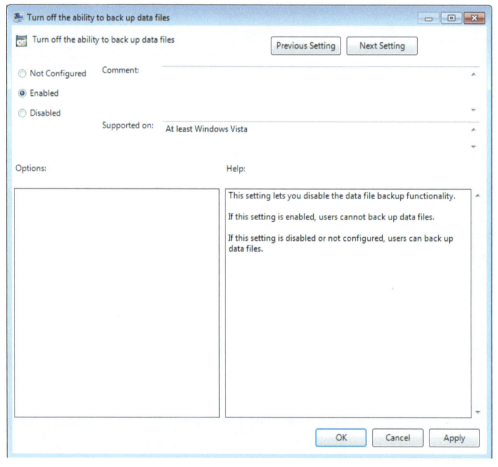

7. Click **Ok** button to accept and confirm your configuration and close **Local Group Policy Editor** snap-in.

8. Open **Command Prompt** and the command window type **GPUPDATE /FORCE** to update your computer with latest settings.

9. Close **Command Prompt**.

Disable Restore Feature

Backups can serve no good and are of no use until they are restorable. This means that even if data has been backed up, till the time it is not recoverable or restorable it has no value. Keeping this in consideration administrators in some cases might want to disable restore feature on a Windows 7 computer. The reason behind this can be that even if a person manages to take the backup of the computer, he should not be able to restore it in order to misuse the system or data. As an administrator you can disable restore feature on a Windows 7 computer by following the steps given below:

1. Log on to the computer with administrator account.

2. Click **Start** button.

3. At the bottom of start menu in search box type **GPEDIT.MSC** and press enter key.

4. On **Local Group Policy Editor** snap-in under **Computer Configuration** expand **Administrative Templates** and expand **Windows Components**.

5. Expand **Backup** and click **Client**.

6. In the right pane, double click **Turn off restore functionality** and in the opened window select **Enabled** radio button.

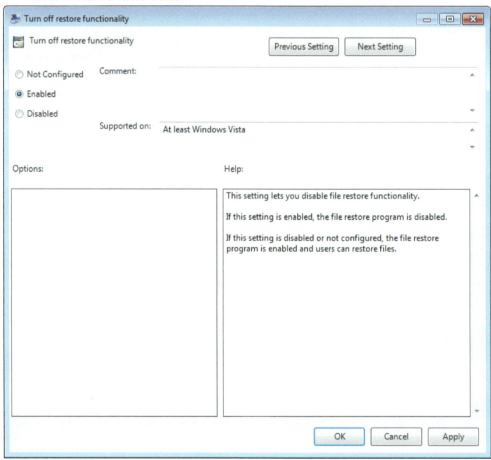

7. Click **Ok** button to accept and confirm your configuration and close **Local Group Policy Editor** snap-in.

8. Open **Command Prompt** and the command window type **GPUPDATE /FORCE** to update your computer with latest settings.

9. Close **Command Prompt**.

Specify a Roaming Profile Path for All Users

In earlier days configuring a roaming profile for all users in a single go was only possible in active directory domain environments. However with latest amendments setting roaming profile path for all users in a single go is possible on a computer that is part of workgroup as well. In order to configure roaming profile for users on a Windows 7 computer it is essential that you have another computer connected to the network and that computer must have a shared folder that can be accessed from anywhere. Once these prerequisites are met you can configure roaming profiles for all users on a Windows 7 computer by following the steps given below:

1. Log on to the computer with administrator account.
2. Click **Start** button.
3. At the bottom of start menu in search box type **GPEDIT.MSC** and press enter key.
4. On **Local Group Policy Editor** snap-in under **Computer Configuration** expand **Administrative Templates** and expand **System**.
5. From the list click **User Profiles** and from the right pane double click **Set roaming profile path for all users from logging onto this computer**..

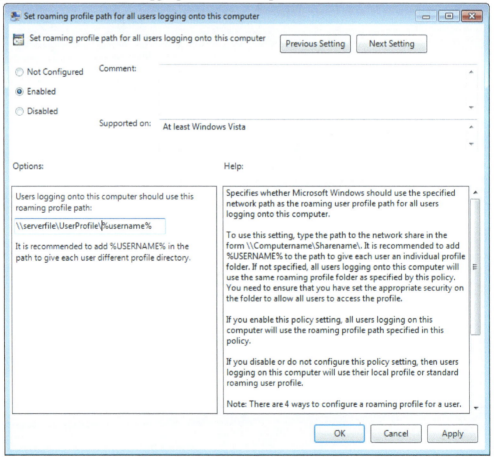

6. On the opened box select **Enabled** radio button and in the **Options** pane specify the roaming profile path (which is the network path of the shared folder on the other computer and is connected to this computer via local area network connection followed by the variable to create user specific folder, e.g. **\\FILESERVER\SHAREDFOLDER\ <USERNAME>.**)

7. Once done, click **Ok** button to accept and confirm your configuration and close **Local Group Policy Editor** snap-in.

8. Open **Command Prompt** and the command window type **GPUPDATE /FORCE** to update your computer with latest settings.

9. Close **Command Prompt**.

Remove Pictures Folder from Start Menu

In any production environment administrators never want users to use office computers for their personal tasks and multimedia purposes. This is the reason why most of them apply various security measures either on every computer (in workup environments) or through domain wide group policies (in domain environments). By following the steps given below you can remove Pictures folder from the start menu so that no user can save his/her personal pictures on a Windows 7 computer.

1. Log on to the computer using administrator account.
2. Click **Start** button.
3. At the bottom of start menu in search box type **GPEDIT.MSC** command and press enter key.
4. From **Local Group Policy Editor** snap-in under **User Configuration** expand **Administrative Templates** and from the list click **Start Menu and Taskbar**.
5. From the right pane double click **Remove Pictures icon from Start Menu**.
6. On **Remove Pictures icon from Start Menu** box select **Enabled** radio button and click **Ok** button to accept and confirm your configuration.

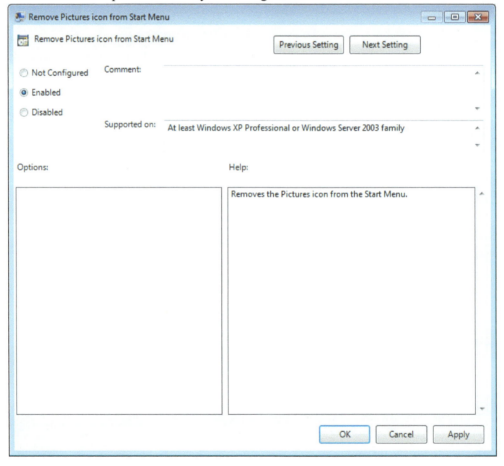

7. Close **Local Group Policy Editor** snap-in and open **Command Prompt**.

8. On the opened command window type **GPUPDATE /FORCE** command and press enter key to update your computer with latest configuration.

9. Close **Command Prompt**.

More Info:

In order to bring Pictures folder back in start menu you need to follow all the above steps except clicking on Disabled in step 6.

Turn Off Aero Shake

Windows 7 has a unique feature which allows users to minimize all opened but inactive Windows when the active window is shaken using mouse button. This feature is new in Windows 7 and is quite helpful for new users as they need not to click Minimize button several times to minimize all opened Windows. Moreover this feature also works on toggle system which means that when the active window is shaken once, all inactive windows are automatically minimized and when the active window is shaken for the second time all minimized Windows are automatically restored. By default Aero Shake is enabled in Windows 7 and only works when Aero theme is enabled. Users can enable or disable this if they want you manage this feature while using Windows. As a Windows 7 user if you want to manage Aero Shake feature you are required to follow the steps given below:

1. Log on to Windows 7 computer with administrator account.

2. At the bottom of start menu in search box type **GPEDIT.MSC** and press enter key.

3. On **User Account Control** confirmation box click **Yes** button.

4. On **Local Group Policy Editor** snap-in under **User Configuration** expand **Administrative Templates** and then click **Desktop** from the left pane.

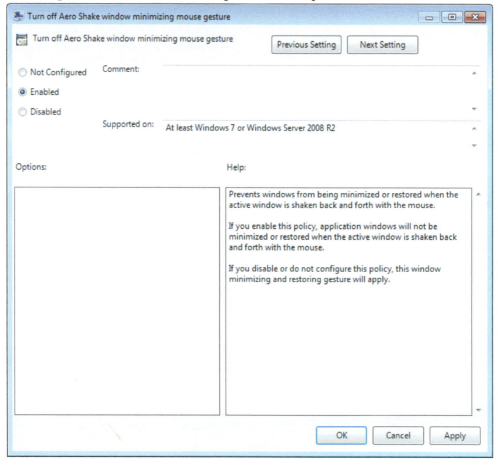

5. From the right pane double-click **Turn off Aero Shake window minimizing mouse gesture** and on the opened box select **Enabled** or **Disabled** radio button to enable or disable **Aero Shake** respectively. Default setting, which is **Not Configured** can also be left intact to keep the feature enabled.

6. Finally click **Ok** button and close the opened snap-in.

Turn Off Windows Explorer Search History

As a Windows 7 user you might be using search feature provided with the operating system every now and then. Also in many cases you may not want any other user to figure out what did you search and when. When this is the case administrators can disable the memory of search. The process requires some group policy editing which can only be done with the account that has administrative privileges. As an administrator of a Windows 7 computer if you want to disable Windows Explorer search memory you are required to follow the steps given as below:

1. Log on to Windows 7 computer with elevated account.

2. Click **Start** button at the bottom of start menu in search box type **GPEDIT.MSC** command and press enter key.

3. On **Local Group Policy Editor** snap-in under **User Configuration** expand **Administrative Templates** and then expand **Windows Components**.

4. From the available list click **Windows Explorer** from the left pane and from the right pane double-click **Turn off display of recent search entries in Windows Explorer search box**.

5. On the opened box click **Enabled** radio button.

6. Click **Ok** button to save the changes that you have made.

7. Open **Command Prompt** and type **GPUPDATE /FORCE** command and press enter key to allow the changes to take effect.

Restrict Users from Shutting Down Windows

By-default any Microsoft client operating system allows all users to shut down the computer. This configuration however might not be appropriate in many cases because of security reasons. Therefore in order to restrict users from shutting down the system, an administrator of a computer can modify the default configuration by changing the settings in group policies. As an administrator you can configure this by following the steps given below:

1. Log on to the computer with administrator's account.

2. Click **Start** button.

3. At the bottom of start menu in search box type **GPEDIT.MSC** command and press enter key.

4. On **Local Computer Policy** snap in under **Computer Configuration** expand **Windows Settings**.

5. From the list expand **Security Settings**.

6. Expand **Local Policies** and click **User Rights Assignment**.

7. From the right pane double click **Shut down the system.**

8. On **Shut down the system Properties** box click on the name of the user or group you want to restrict and click on **Remove** button.

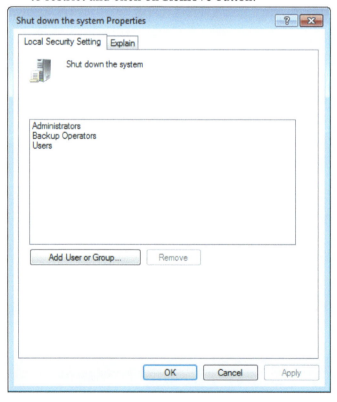

9. Click **Ok** button to confirm your configuration and close **Local Group Policy** snap-in.

10. Open **Command Prompt** and in the command window type **GPUPDATE /FORCE** command to update the computer with new group policy settings.

11. Close command window.

Disable Task Manager

When a Windows 7 computer is used in home environments its default configuration is mostly considered as ideal. However in production environments administrators always want to make it as secure as possible. To add another layer of security on Windows 7 computer administrators should disable Task Manager for all users. If you are an administrator you can disable Task Manager by following the steps given below:

1. Log on to the computer with administrator account.

2. Click **Start** button.

3. At the bottom of start menu in search box type **GPEDIT.MSC** command and press enter key.

4. On the opened **Local Group Policy Editor** snap-in under **User Configuration** expand **Administrative Templates** and then expand **System**.

5. Click **Ctrl+Alt+Del** Options and from the right pane double click **Remove Task Manager**.

6. On the opened box select **Enabled** radio button and click **Ok** button to accept your configuration.

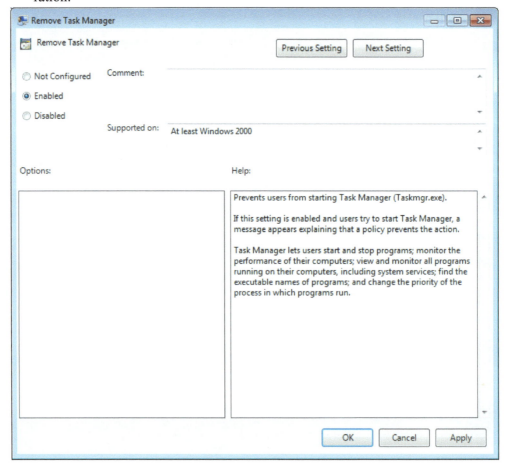

7. Close **Local Group Policy Editor** snap-in and open **Command Prompt**.

8. On the command window type **GPUPDATE /FORCE** command to update your current computer configuration with latest settings.

9. Close **Command Prompt.**

Real World Scenario Tip:

Sometimes due to virus infections Task Manager automatically gets disabled. When this happens the above process can be reversed in order to re-enable Task Manager. If Task Manager is disabled due to virus infection and in group policy settings its status is Not Configured, you first need to disable it and then enable it. Finally you can change the settings back to Not Configured in order to get the default settings of Task Manager back.

Prevent Default Windows Sound Modifications

As default nature of Microsoft Windows 7, users can modify system sound settings for their profiles so that they may enjoy sounds other than default Windows Sound scheme. For home users this configuration is ideal and needs not to be modified under normal circumstances. However in medium to large scale organizations administrators would want to restrict users from modifying default Windows Sound settings for various reasons. As an administrator you can restrict users from doing so by following the steps given below:

1. Log on to the Windows 7 computer using administrator account.

2. Click **Start** button.

3. At the bottom of start menu in search box type **GPEDIT.MSC** and press enter key.

4. From the opened **Local Group Policy Editor** snap-in under **User Configuration** expand **Administrative Templates** and expand **Control Panel**.

5. Click on **Personalization** and from the right pane double click **Prevent changing sounds**.

6. On **Prevent changing sounds** box click **Enabled** radio button and click **Ok** button to accept and confirm your configuration.

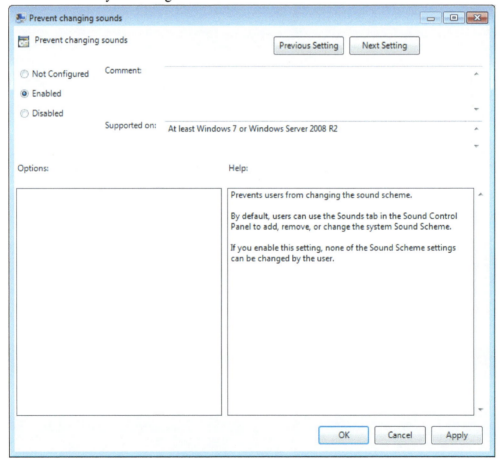

7. Close **Local Group Policy Editor** snap-in and open **Command Prompt**.

8. In the command window type **GPUPDATE /FORCE** command and press enter key to update the latest configuration on your Windows 7 computer.

9. Close **Command Prompt**.

More Info:

In order allow users to change default sound scheme you need to follow all the above steps except selecting **Disabled** or **Not Configured** radio button on **step 6**.

Clear Pagefile While Shutting Down

Pagefile is the virtual memory where information is stored when the RAM is full. Although the information stored in pagefile is encrypted and cannot be decrypted easily, to add an extra layer of security many administrators may want to erase the sensitive information in virtual memory when the computer shuts down in order to protect it from getting stolen and misused. As an administrator if you want to clear the sensitive information stored in pagefile you need to follow the steps given below:

1. Log on to the computer with administrator account.

2. Click **Start** button.

3. At bottom of start menu in search box type **GPEDIT.MSC** command and press enter key.

4. On **Local Group Policy Editor** snap-in under **Computer Configuration** expand **Windows Settings** and then expand **Security Settings**.

5. Expand **Local Policies** and click **Security Options**.

6. From the right pane double click **Shutdown: Clear virtual memory pagefile** and on the opened box select **Enabled** radio button.

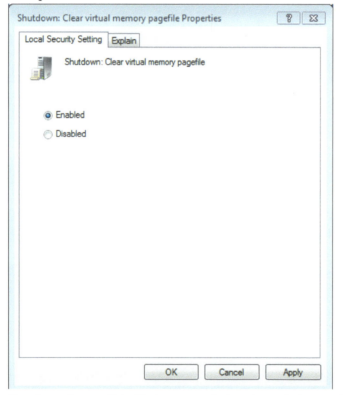

7. Once done, click **Ok** button and close **Local Group Policy Editor** snap-in.

8. Open **Command Prompt** and in command window type **GPUPDATE /FORCE** to update here computer policy with latest configuration.

9. Close **Command Prompt**.

Enable Search Box to Search Internet

Windows 7 has a great feature named Search Box which is available at the bottom of start menu. Search Box is capable of finding any object in indexed form, which means that the search is instantaneous and real-time. This further means that the objects can be located as users start typing their names. However many administrators and users do not know that Search Box can also be configured to search Internet contents right from itself. This configuration requires elevated privileges and as an administrator of a Windows 7 computer if you want to configure Search Box to find Internet contents, you are required to follow the steps given below:

1. Log on to the computer with administrator account.
2. At the bottom of start menu in search box type **GPEDIT.MSC** command and press enter key.
3. On the opened **Local Group Policy Editor** snap-in under **User Configuration** expand **Administrative Templates** and then click **Start Menu and Taskbar** from the left pane.
4. From the right pane double-click **Add Search Internet link to Start Menu** and from the opened box select **Enabled** radio button.

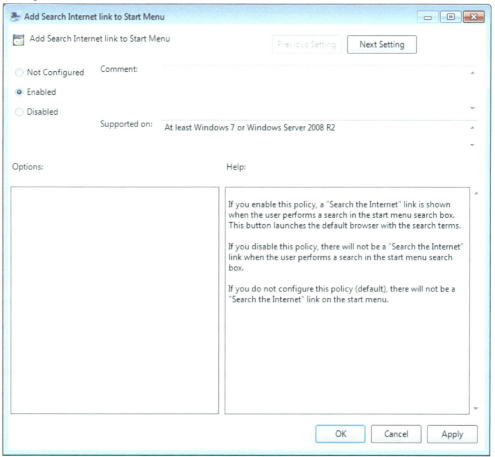

5. Once done, click **Ok** button to save the changes and in **Command Prompt** type **GPUP-DATE /FORCE** command to allow the changes to take effect.

Printer Sharing

Installing shared printers on every computer of the network might be quite hectic for both administrators and users. In earlier days administrators used group policies to configure startup/shutdown or logon/log-off scripts to deploy shared printers to the computers and/or users automatically. This practice required batch files to be created and commands to be written to solve the purpose. However in Windows server 2008 and Windows 7 operating systems Microsoft has integrated a new group policy feature named Deployed Printers in order to reduce administrative overhead and expedite the printer deployment process. As an administrator you can deploy shared printers automatically throughout the network with single configuration by following the steps given below:

1. Log on to the computer with administrator account and in the search box available in start menu type **GPEDIT.MSC** and press enter.

2. In the opened snap-in under **Computer Configuration** expand **Windows Settings**.

3. From the expanded list right click **Deployed Printers** and from the appeared menu choose **Deploy Printer** option.

4. On **Deploy Printer(s)** box click **Browse** button to locate the shared printer available anywhere in your network and once found click **Add** button to add the printer to the list.

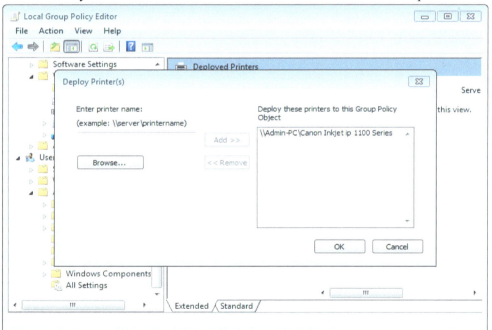

5. Once done, click **Ok** button to accept the configuration and finally close the opened snap-in.

6. Use **GPUPDATE /FORCE** in command prompt to update your computer settings with the latest configuration.

Note: This policy configuration can be exploited best in client server architecture where entire network infrastructure is centrally managed.

Disable "Found New Hardware" Balloon

In Windows 7 whenever a new device is connected or whenever the operating system finds that a new hardware is attached to the computer, it displays a balloon in the notification area saying "Found New Hardware". In home environment this notification proves quite handy as users may know that any device is attached, which further helps them take appropriate action in that regard. However in production environments sometimes administrators may not want this notification to appear on desktop PCs for various security reasons. As an administrator you can disable this balloon from appearing in front of users by following the steps given below:

1. Log on to the computer with administrator account.
2. Click **Start** button.
3. At the bottom of start menu in search box type **GPEDIT.MSC** and press enter key.
4. On **Local Group Policy Editor** snap-in under **Computer Configuration** expand **Administrative Templates** and expand **System**.
5. From expanded list select **Device Installation** from the right pane double click **Turn off New Hardware Found balloons during device installation** and on the opened window select **Enabled** radio button.

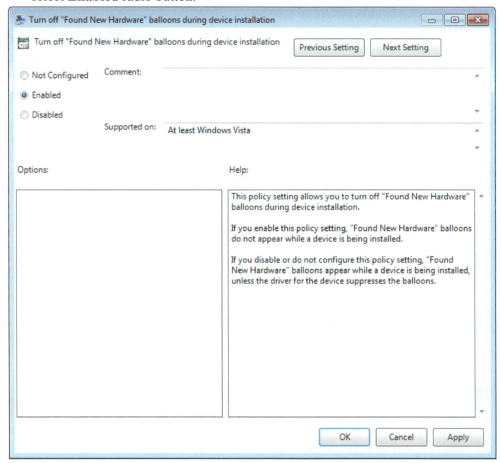

6. Once done click **Ok** button to accept and confirm your configuration.

7. Close **Local Group Policy Editor** snap-in and open **Command Prompt**.

8. In command window type **GPUPDATE /FORCE** and press enter key to update your computer configuration with latest settings.

9. Close **Command Prompt**.

Disable All Balloon Notifications

With the release of Microsoft Windows 7 operating system, notifications to the users given by the machine have also been modified and have been made even more efficient so that users need not to wander around all over the computer to find the updated information regarding anything. Although notifications play an important role as far as updates of the operating system are concerned however sometimes these notifications can become annoying for the users who are not technically sound. When this is the case many administrators of computers may want to disable notification balloons in Windows 7 so that they can cause no more nuisances to the users. As an administrator of a Windows 7 computer in any home environment if you want to disable notification balloons you are required to follow the steps given below:

1. Log on to Windows 7 computer with the account that has administrative privileges.
2. Click **Start** button and at the bottom of the available menu in search box type **GPEDIT.MSC** and press enter.
3. On **Local Group Policy Editor** snap-in under **User Configuration** expand **Administrative Templates** and from the available list click **Start Menu and Taskbar** from the left pane.
4. From the right pane double-click **Turn off all balloon notifications**.

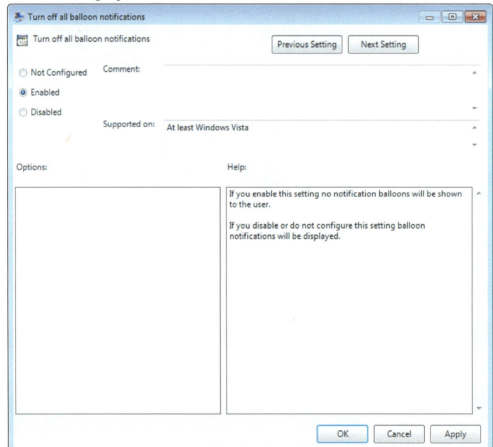

5. On the opened box click **Enable** radio button to select and finally click **Ok** button to save the changes that you have made.

6. If required, restart your computer.

Manage Device Installation Errors

While installing device drivers in Windows 7 errors might occur only because of two possible reasons. Either device driver is not compatible with the hardware attached to the machine or the installation process of device driver is taking long enough to enforce installation to terminate. The first possibility can only be managed by getting a copy of device driver that actually belongs to the attached device. However in later case administrators can increase the time-out duration of device installation in order to provide sufficient time for the installation process to complete. As an administrator you can do so by following the steps given below:

1. Log on to the computer with administrator account.
2. Click **Start** button.
3. At the bottom of start menu in search box type **GPEDIT.MSC** and press enter key.
4. On **Local Group Policy Editor** snap-in under **Computer Configuration** expand **Administrative Templates** and expand **System**.
5. From expanded list select **Device Installation** from the right pane double click **Configure device installation time-out**.

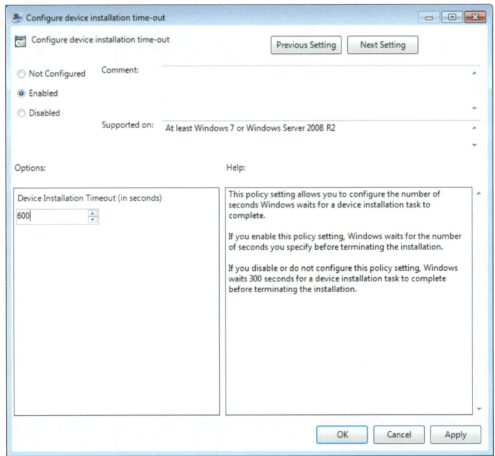

6. On the opened window select **Enabled** radio button and in the **Options** in the available space specify the time-out duration in seconds. (Default is 300 sec).

7. Once done click **Ok** button to accept and confirm your configuration.

8. Close **Local Group Policy Editor** snap-in and open **Command Prompt**.

9. In command window type **GPUPDATE /FORCE** and press enter key to update your computer configuration with latest settings.

10. Close **Command Prompt**.

Import/Export Security Policies

Configuring security in Windows 7 computer is a time taking process. Administrators spend their lot of time struggling with Security Settings offered by Windows group policies. Once security settings are configured, administrators move on to the next computer to repeat the process. This practice consumes lot of energy and time which is not feasible for production environments. The process becomes even more hectic while working with workgroup network setups. However to remarkably reduce administrators' overhead Microsoft allows them to export completely configure security settings in an .inf file which can then be imported on to another computer to configure exactly the same settings on it. Process of exporting and importing security policies is quite simple and as an administrator you can follow the steps given below to do so:

1. Since only administrators can perform this task, log on to your computer with administrator account and at the bottom of start menu in search box type **GPEDIT.MSC** command and hit enter.

2. In the opened snap-in under **Computer Configuration** expand **Windows Settings** and from the expanded list right click **Security Settings**.

3. From the appeared menu choose **Export policy** to export the entire security configuration. (The security considerations will be saved in an .inf file and can be saved at your desired location).

4. Once done, click **Ok** button to close the opened snap-in.

Note: In order to import the exported security policy you need to log on to the target computer with administrator's account and follow the steps exactly as mentioned above. However in order to import you need to choose Import policy in the third step rather than selecting Export policy.

Specify When Windows Checks for Updates

In production environments where there are several computers connected to a single local area network and share a common Internet connection, Windows Server Update Services server is configured to make latest updates available to the clients on the local intranet. Since working offline expedites every task, administrators may also want to decrease the time interval between two subsequent update searches that Windows 7 computers make. This ensures that client computers are always up-to-date with latest updates and patches and are secured. As an administrator, you can configure this by following the steps given below:

1. Log on to the computer using administrator account.

2. Click **Start** button.

3. At the bottom of start menu in search box type **GPEDIT.MSC** and press enter key.

4. From the **Local Group Policy Editor** snap-in under **Computer Configuration** expand **Administrative Templates** and then expand **Windows Components**.

5. From the expanded list select **Windows Update** and from the right pane double click **Automatic Updates detection frequency**.

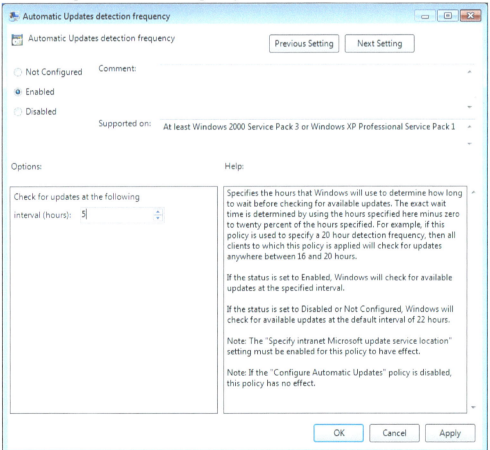

6. From the opened box, select **Enabled** radio button and under **Options** section in **Interval hours** text box specify the time interval.

7. Click **Ok** button to accept and confirm you selection and close **Local Group Policy Editor** snap-in.

8. Open **Command Prompt**.

9. In command window type **GPUPDATE /FORCE** and press enter key to update your computer with latest settings.

10. Close **Command Prompt**.

Use Power Management for Automatic Updates

By default when Windows is in hibernation state it does not wake up when Automatic Updates is scheduled and latest updates are available. This feature, though, is not a problem when used in homes. However when Windows 7 computer is used in production environments and when latest updates are available, it becomes essential for the operating systems to receive them in order to make computers secure as soon as possible. To accomplish this task, administrators need to ensure that systems are up and running when automatic updates are scheduled and are available. Latest feature helps administrators in this regard. Administrators can now use Windows Power Management feature to enforce computers wake up when automatic updates are scheduled and are available. Administrators can configure this by following the steps given below:

1. Log on to the computer using administrator account.
2. Click **Start** button.
3. At the bottom of start menu in search box type **GPEDIT.MSC** and press enter key.
4. From the **Local Group Policy Editor** snap-in under **Computer Configuration** expand **Administrative Templates** and then expand **Windows Components**.

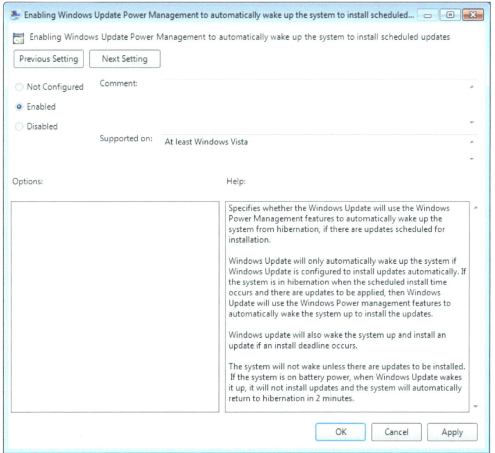

5. From the expanded list select **Windows Update** and from the right pane double click **Enabling Windows Update Power Management to automatically wake up the system to install scheduled updates**.

6. From the opened box select **Enabled** radio button and click **Ok** button to accept and confirm you selection.

7. Close **Local Group Policy Editor** snap-in and open **Command Prompt**.

8. In command window type **GPUPDATE /FORCE** and press enter key to update your computer with latest settings.

9. Close **Command Prompt**.

Disable Driver Search on Windows Update Site

Whenever a device is attached to a Windows 7 computer, the operating system prompts for the location from where Windows should download and install the latest device drivers. According to the attached device, administrators can choose appropriate options from the available list. However in some cases where administrators always know that they would not look out for device drivers on Microsoft update server they can configure their Windows 7 computers react accordingly. As an administrator if you want to specify this configuration you need follow the steps given below:

1. Log on to the computer with administrator account.

2. Click **Start** button.

3. At the bottom of start menu in search box type **GPEDIT.MSC** and press enter key.

4. On **Local Group Policy Editor** snap-in under **Computer Configuration** expand **Administrative Templates** and expand **System**.

5. From expanded list select **Device Installation** and from the right pane double click **Specify search order for device driver source locations.**

6. On the opened window select **Enabled** radio button and in the **Options** section from the drop-down list choose **Do not search Windows Update**.

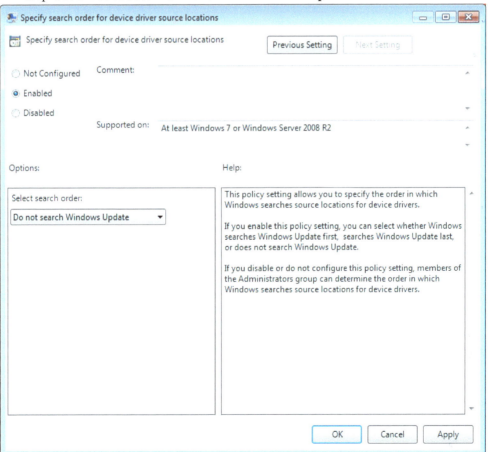

7. Once done click **Ok** button to accept and confirm your configuration.

8. Close **Local Group Policy Editor** snap-in and open **Command Prompt**.

9. In command window type **GPUPDATE /FORCE** and press enter key to update your computer configuration with latest settings.

10. Close **Command Prompt**.

Automatic Windows Updates through WSUS

By-default Windows 7 is configured to receive automatic updates from Microsoft update server. For home users this configuration might be quite ideal as there is only one or two computers connected to the internet. However in production environments where there are several computers and all share a common Internet connection, downloading Windows updates for every machine directly from the Internet might result in reduced internet performance and speed. In order to eliminate this problem administrators usually configure Windows Server Update Services (WSUS) server which connects to the Microsoft update server and downloads all available updates related to the computers present in the offices. Computers, which in this case are Windows 7 PCs, then connect to the Windows Server Update Service server and download and install latest updates from there. This saves considerable amount of time and internet bandwidth. To use WSUS server as Windows Update Server, Windows 7 computers are required to be configured through group policies to do so. Process to do so is given below:

1. Log on to the computer using administrator account.
2. Click **Start** button.
3. At the bottom of start menu in search box type **GPEDIT.MSC** and press enter key.
4. From the **Local Group Policy Editor** snap-in under **Computer Configuration** expand **Administrative Templates** and then expand **Windows Components**.
5. From the expanded list select **Windows Update** and from the right pane double click **Specify intranet Microsoft update service location**.
6. From the opened box select **Enabled** radio button and under **Options** section and type the URL address of WSUS server available on the intranet.
7. Click **Ok** button to accept and confirm you selection and close **Local Group Policy Editor** snap-in.
8. Open **Command Prompt**.
9. In command window type **GPUPDATE /FORCE** and press enter key to update your computer with latest settings.
10. Close **Command Prompt**

More Info:

In domain environments, this configuration is mostly managed through Default Domain Group Policy GPO or any other GPO, which is precisely created for the purpose.

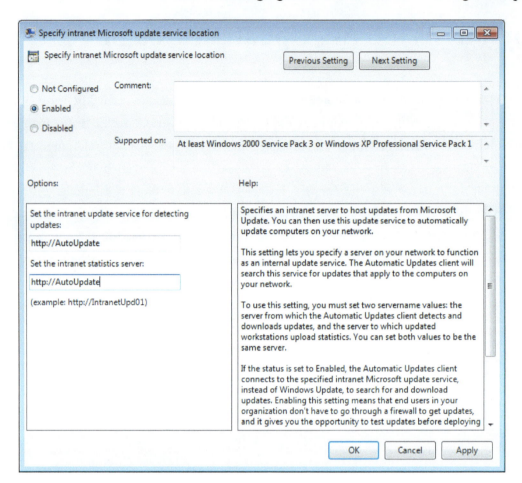